P9-DNV-867

THE PRIVATE LIFE OF
PLANTS

David Attenborough

THE PRIVATE LIFE OF
PLANTS

A Natural History of Plant Behaviour

PRINCETON UNIVERSITY PRESS
PRINCETON, NEW JERSEY

Published in the United States by Princeton University Press,
41 William Street, Princeton, New Jersey 08540

Frontispiece: the titan arum flowering in the
tropical rain forest of Sumatra (see pages 134-40)

© David Attenborough Productions Ltd. 1995

ISBN 0-691-00639-3

Library of Congress Cataloging-in-Publication Data

A CIP catalog record for this book is available from
the Library of Congress

A Domino book. All rights reserved. No part of this
publication may be reproduced, stored in a retrieval system, or
transmitted in any form or by any means without permission
from Domino Books Ltd., 7 Bond Street, St Helier, Jersey

Printed and bound by the Bath Press, Glasgow and Bath

CONTENTS

INTRODUCTION

Plants can see. They can count and communicate with one another. They are able to react to the slightest touch and to estimate time with extraordinary precision.

Such statements, put baldly, seem almost fanciful not to say exaggerated to the point of falsity. Yet while some of these abilities have only recently been identified by botanists, the evidence for others is known to anyone who has the slightest acquaintance with plants – and that must surely mean almost everyone.

A shoot kept in the dark will creep towards a single chink of light. The plant can see. Hedgerow flowers facing west at sunset, turn during the night to face east to catch the dawn sun and will continue to make such movements even when kept under uniform lighting for days on end. They can estimate time. The Venus flytrap closes when its trigger hair is touched not once but twice. It can count.

Furthermore, plants, during the course of their lives must grapple with much the same problems as animals, including ourselves. They must fight their enemies. They have to struggle with their neighbours to claim space in which to live and gather their food. They take other organisms captive and use them for their own purposes. And they compete with one another for mates.

The reason that most of us are largely unaware of these dramas and the powers and sensitivities of the protagonists is, I suspect, largely because plants live on a different time-scale than we do. Today, however, the ever-expanding technology of film and video enables us to modify time visually and speed up movement. Actions of plants that are imperceptible to our steady gaze become immediately and obviously visible and we can then appreciate very well the ferocity with which a strangler fig squeezes the life from its victims, the determination with which a mistletoe seedling plugs its root into the branch of a tree, as well as the languorous grace with which an orchid unfurls its complex blooms.

The television programmes on which I was working at the same time as I was writing this book, were able to reveal the personalities and activities of plants in this way. It has been my aim to maintain that attitude here. In doing so, however, I do not wish to suggest that plants have the same kind of consciousness as higher animals have. There is no evidence of that being so and nothing in the pages that follow should be taken to suggest the contrary. Nor do I intend to imply that plants are able to determine their own evolutionary ends, that an orchid *decides* to impersonate a female wasp in order to induce a male wasp to try and copulate with it and thus become saddled with the orchid's pollen. There is no evidence for this either. The only accepted evolutionary force that could bring about such a phenomenon is natural selection, as proposed originally by Charles Darwin.

Botany, like all other sciences, has its own jargon, its own specialist vocabulary with its own precise meanings and therefore its own value to those who have been initiated into its disciplines. Such language can be at best baffling and at worst off-putting to non-botanists, and I have therefore avoided technical terms wherever possible. The price of doing so has been, in some contexts, a loss of scientific precision. This is particularly the case when using popular names for species of plants instead of scientific ones. I have tried to compensate for this, to some extent, by making the index serve as a glossary. Thus if a reader should wish to know precisely what a plant name refers to, it can be discovered by looking it up in the index. The first word of a scientific name is that of an organism's genus – its surname, as it were. The second is that which identifies a particular species. The pitcher plant genus is *Nepenthes* and it contains over sixty species. If the text is referring to pitcher plants in general, that name in the index will be followed by *Nepenthes* sp. If the text refers to the twin-spurred pitcher plant, then the index will reveal that scientifically this is *Nepenthes bicalcarata*.

If plants have no accepted English name, I have referred to them by their generic name but without printing it in italics or even capitalising it. This may seem unforgivably heretical to some, but in fact horticulture has been doing the same thing for a very long time. For a gardening article these days to capitalise and italicise the names delphinium or fuchsia would be somewhat pedantic. I hope, therefore, that I may be forgiven if in the cause of easier reading I have used the same style for banksia and tibouchina.

Plants are, in many ways, much more successful organisms than animals. They were the first to colonise the land on this planet. Even today, they can thrive in places where no animal can exist for any length of time. They grow much bigger than any animal and they live much longer. And animals are totally dependant upon them. As the Old Testament puts it so pithily, all flesh is grass. All animals, including the most determined of carnivores, eat plants, if not first-hand, then at second, third or fourth. The Inuit of the Arctic, who used to be known as the Eskimo, were reputed, before they took to softer southern ways, to have existed entirely on the flesh of seals and fish and to eat no vegetables whatever. Yet seals eat fish, fish eat small fish, and they in turn eat smaller creatures such as tiny shrimps, which themselves graze on vast clouds of microscopic algae, floating in the surface waters of the oceans. Algae are plants. All flesh is indeed grass.

We may, in the face of such irrefutable facts, recognise our dependence on plants. We are not so ready to concede that our dominance over them is anything less than total. We do, after all, exploit them not only for food but for warmth, clothing, as building material, even for decoration. We uproot and lop them, germinate and transplant them, largely as we wish. It seldom occurs to us, as we pick a burr from our socks or drink another glass of wine, that we are actors in strategies that were initiated not by ourselves but by them, strategies that have been hugely successful in their campaigns to claim ever more living space on earth for their species.

This book is an attempt to see the natural world, not from our point of view, but from theirs.

1

TRAVELLING

ALL PLANTS must travel. Swiftly moving creatures such as ourselves tend to regard them as immobile organisms, leading stationary lives, rooted to the ground. But the lives of plants, like our own and those of all other animals, culminate in the production of more individuals of their own kind which will try to claim space for themselves and so extend the dominion of their species. And to do that, plants – at some stage in their lives – have to travel.

Some manage to do so as adults. One of the most mobile of plants in an English woodland is the blackberry. An individual, once established, immediately starts to seek new territory for itself. It puts out exploratory stems. They spring from the central root stock, curving upwards and out, their tips waving slowly from side to side as though they are searching. If they touch the stem of another plant or any other object, their motion changes. They begin to advance directly and purposefully. Their motion is not visible to our unaided eye even though, for plants, it is extraordinarily fast – about two inches a day. But their actions, when revealed by the time-lapse camera, are alarmingly aggressive. Each stem is armed with sharp backward-pointing spines which catch on the ground and snag on vegetation. They clamber over logs and up the faces of rocks. They reach up, hook onto the stems of other plants and scramble over them, overwhelming them. Every now and then, in places where its stems make contact with the ground, the invader secures its gains by putting down small rootlets and so starts immediately to extract nutriment from its newly-acquired territory. Few animals will manage to displace it, for the spines which served so well during the invasion now constitute a formidable defence capable of giving

◁
*The aggressive
blackberry plant
advances over an
English hedgerow*

nasty wounds to intruding paws, muzzles or hands. The blackberry has established its empire.

Other plant imperialists look more innocuous but are equally effective. In ditches and along roadsides, the silverweed also extends its holdings by putting out travelling stems. They are not armed and do not arch through the air as dramatically as the blackberry. Instead they advance horizontally, close to the ground and creep surreptitiously through the mat of rootlets and dead vegetation formed by other plants. At intervals, from joints in those stems, it sprouts leaves and, like the blackberry, puts down rootlets.

Out in the meadows, fescue grass grows in a similar way, annexing land from other less robust and aggressive species. The genetic fingerprints of its leaves and stems taken two hundred yards apart in a meadow have proved, in some instances, to be identical. This must mean that one particularly vigorous plant has maintained its dominance and increased its territory year after year until now, after perhaps a century, it has come to dominate the entire meadow. That entitles the fescue to be ranked not only as one of the longest-lived of all herbaceous plants but one of the largest.

In the deserts of the American west, another adult plant makes even longer journeys. The bird-cage plant grows among the sand dunes, in corners where there is a little shade, where it has a chance of putting down long roots to search for water, and where it is able to gather a little moisture from the infrequent morning dews. But dunes move and what may have been once a favourable site for a plant may overnight become an untenable one. The shifting sand may have blown away to expose the roots; the slope that once shaded it may have disappeared, exposing the plant to an intolerable intensity of sunshine. Under such stress the plant dies. Its roots shrivel. The stems radiating from its centre curl upwards and transform the plant into a hollow spherical lattice the size of an orange. The wind now catches it. With no roots to anchor it, it bowls over the sand. It leaps and bounces up the steep dune faces and races along the downward slopes. It may travel for days, mile after mile.

But eventually, it rolls into a corner where the wind can no longer find it. It has discovered a sheltered site where conditions are much more tolerable. For the traveller itself, the improvement has come too late. It is dead. But within its lattice there is life – inside the pods.

◁
Silverweed sends out colonising runners

Seeds may have been spilling from them during the long journey. Those are likely to have been wasted. But now, in this new sheltered position, they tumble out in greater numbers as heat splits open the pods, and these seeds will have a much better chance of germination and survival.

The withered seed-carrying body of a bird-cage plant comes to rest in the dunes of California
▽

Seeds contain all the genetic information necessary to reproduce their parents. In addition, most also carry a store of nutriment that will sustain the young seedling during its first stages of growth until it is able to start manufacturing food for itself. Yet all this is contained within a speck that may be smaller than a sand-grain. And precisely because seeds are so small and therefore so easily shifted, they are the form in which the majority of plants do most of their travelling.

One or two plants, with splendid independence, seek no help from anything, animate or inanimate. They distribute their seeds using entirely their own forces. The little Mediterranean squirting cucumber, as it ripens, fills with a slimy juice. Eventually, the pressure within becomes so great that the cucumber bursts off its stalk and shoots through the air for as far as twenty feet. Behind it, streaming from the hole in its base like gases flaring behind a space rocket, comes a trail of slime and with it, seeds.

As it ripens, the Mediterranean squirting cucumber fills its seed-pods with liquid
▽

◁
*The exploding
seed-pods of broom*

Broom powers its explosions in exactly the opposite manner. Its launching energy comes not from an increase of liquid but from its evaporation. As a pod warms on a summer's day, the side facing the sun dries faster than that in the shade. This sets up a tension in the pod which finally causes it to split suddenly into its two halves, caterpulting its tiny black seeds in all directions as it does so. The most dramatic of such detonating seed-containers belongs to a Brazilian tree. Its botanical name is Hura, but it is sometimes engagingly known as monkey's dinner-bell. When it dries out and finally explodes, it hurls its seeds for distances of over forty feet and the bang it makes as it does so is quite enough to convince nervous strangers in the forest that they are under attack.

Some seeds are so tiny that, equipped with even the simplest of apparatus, they can be carried by the wind. Kapok trees and cotton bushes do no more than provide each of their seeds with a tuft of threads. These are so long and so strong that we ourselves use them for making textiles and as packing materials. They serve the seeds by simply catching the wind and they do so with such effect that seed can be carried for miles.

The dandelion provides its seeds with a slightly more complex flying apparatus, a tiny disc of radiating threads that form, in effect, a parachute. A dandelion presents these seeds to the wind hoisted on the top of a stem and arranged as a fragile elegant globe. Even the gentlest breath, from the wind or a child, can cause squadrons to take off and sail high and far through the sky.

▷
*The seeds of a
dandelion begin
their flight*

Such methods are not very effective within woods, for little wind blows there. A seed with a mop of fine fibres or a little parachute is likely therefore to drop more or less directly to the ground and come to rest unsuitably close to its parent's roots. But trees have a special asset to exploit – their height. Fit the seed with a wing and it will travel much farther.

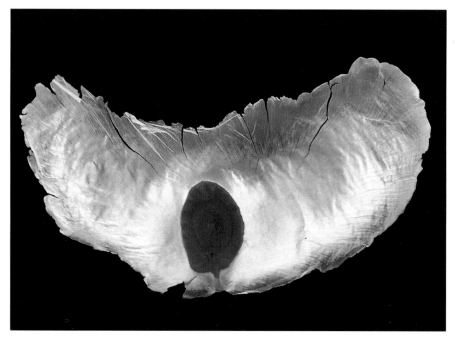

◁
The six-inch-long
gliding seed of
alsomitra

Alsomitra, a liana growing in the tropical forests of Asia, produces its seeds packed together within a pod in sheaves of several hundred. Each is equipped with a wing on its side, which is so paper-thin as to be almost transparent. Although the seed itself is about as heavy as a pea, its wing is so large that the loading is very light, and when the whole glider is released it descends very slowly and is therefore capable of travelling for a hundred yards or more. In fact, it seldom flies such distances as that in the forest. Usually it collides with the branch of another tree in mid-flight. This upsets its balance and the seed tips and flutters down almost directly to the ground.

Anisoptera, one of the tallest of the trees in the same Asiatic forests, also has two wings, but they are spear-shaped and curve upwards and outwards. As its name suggests, they are also unequal in length. This asymmetry causes them to spin when they are released, and the seed resembles a tiny whirling helicopter, which may travel even further than a double-winged glider.

European maples and syca-mores have an even more eco-nomical design. They are equipped with only a single wing, sprouting from one side. The balance between the weight of the seed and the length of the wing is so accu-rately matched that these seeds also spin. Sycamores often grow in relatively isolated locations, and there the wind can give the seeds considerable assistance. Even in a light breeze their tiny spinning helicopters can travel for very long distances across the English countryside.

◇

*The descent of anisoptera's
helicopter seed*
▷

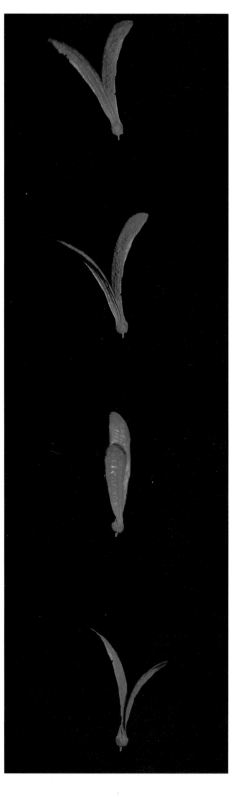

Some trees send their seeds, not by air, but by sea. The most famous of all is the coconut palm. It dispatches its seed inside a hard shell that contains everything needed for a long voyage. Inside there is a supply of rich food, the so-called meat, and a half-a-pint or so of water. On the outside, it is fitted with a fibre float that keeps it on the surface of the water. This survival package serves it so well that coconut palms have colonised beaches throughout the tropics.

▷
The huge pod of the sea-bean hanging above the bank of a South African river

◁
Coconuts germinate after arriving by sea

In some ways, however, the sea-bean is an even more remarkable traveller, for it grows not only on the ocean shores, but on the banks of rivers, in Africa, Australia and South America, many miles from the sea. Its coin-shaped seeds are not as big as coconuts, but they are nonetheless gigantic compared with those of other members of the bean family, for they are about two inches across and carried in gigantic pods four feet long. When they first form, these pods, like other bean pods are green and soft, but as they ripen they become woody and heavy. Eventually, the pod falls into the river beside which the tree is growing and floats away. The pod breaks apart along thin grooves that run across it between the seeds. Each seed, with its own section of pod as packaging, then starts its own individual journey. Some may be stranded on a sand bank or a muddy beach within a few yards of their parents. But others regularly float down the whole length of the river, past the mangrove swamps around its estuary and on out to sea. By the time the seed gets washed up on a beach it may have lost every vestige of its pod, but even after a year at sea, it can still be viable. The sea-bean's transport is so efficient that its seeds occasionally get carried far beyond the reach of the climate in which they can grow successfully. Those launched in the Caribbean are sometimes transported by the Gulf Stream some four thousand miles to Europe where they regularly mystify people taking sea-side holidays who pick them up from the chilly sand.

◁
Sea-beans, stripped of their casing of pod and washed up on a beach

   This part of the sea-bean's story is well known and easy to authenticate. But there must be more to it, for the obvious question arises as to how the seeds get high up a river in the first place. For this there is little evidence, but it is reasonable to suppose that the sea-bean, when making these relatively short up-stream journeys, uses another kind of transport altogether – animals.

◇

△
The fearsome seed-pod of the African grapple plant

Plants recruit animals as carriers in several different ways – by bribery, deceit, self-sacrifice and straightforward coercion. You have only to walk through thick undergrowth in almost any part of the world to discover that you yourself have been exploited. Your trousers, skirts, socks, jerseys, are quite likely to be carrying seeds of one sort or another, attached by long single hooks, or by recurved spines so tiny and dense that the seed looks furry. These burrs and stick-on seeds are irritating to us, and doubtless even more so to hairy animals, – foxes and lions, rabbits, dogs, cattle. They, after all, lack fingers to pick them off and have to get rid of them by rubbing or licking. But some of these hitch-hikers are more than irritating. They can be vicious and inflict serious injuries. The South African grapple plant, a low-growing creeper, relies on its seeds being trodden on. Its capsules have arms ending in hooks that are so sharp, so strong and point in so many directions that when the foot of an elephant or rhino descends on one, the hooks fasten into the sole and the capsule stays there, step after step, until the arm wears so thin that it breaks and the capsule with its seeds breaks away.

◇

△
South African ants hauling the seed of a plant down into their underground nest, in order to eat its coating

Some plants produce seeds that instead of hurting their carriers reward them. This technique is used by a great proportion of the plants that grow in the fynbos, the heathland of South Africa. They provide their seeds with an oily, edible covering called an eliasome. Ants find this particularly attractive. They collect such seeds and carry them down to their underground nests where they take their payment for their transport service by gnawing off the eliasomes. The seeds themselves, full of nutriment though they are, are of no interest to the ants and are abandoned. So the seeds reach an ideal position underground where they can germinate, safely out of the sight and reach of other potential consumers. Indeed, if the seeds are not taken underground by the ants within a few hours of being shed, 99% of them will be eaten in their entirety by mice and other rodents.

There is a riskier way of attracting a carrier. Many plants provide such a generous edible reward, completely enclosing the seed, that the animal-carrier is encouraged to swallow both together. Such packages, of course, are fruits and we succumb to them as enthusiastically as other animals.

Seeds are such complex structures that it takes a plant some time to construct them. The whole strategy would be spoiled if a carrier ate the fruit before the seeds it contains were properly developed. So while this process is still going on, the sap in the fruit's flesh is acid and so sour that the flesh tastes very unpleasant. Any animal that eats it is likely to become quite ill. But once the seeds are fully developed the sap becomes delectably sweet and the fruit signals the fact that the seeds are now ready for transport by changing colour. Apples and strawberries turn from green to red, plums and figs turn purple. Some tropical figs turn pale yellow for they seek the help of night-flying fruit-bats and need to be easily visible in the dark. The colours differ but the message is the same. The animal-carriers understand these signals well. Monkeys feeding in a tree that is only just coming into fruit are as selective in choosing which they will eat as any good housewife in a market, inspecting each fruit closely and lifting it up to their nostrils for a quick sniff before risking a bite.

The smell produced by the fruit reaches a much wider public than a visual signal, even if it is not as precise a guide to an exact location. Who can forget, once having smelled it, the delicious fragrance of figs and peaches ripening under a hot Mediterranean sun? The durian tree of south-east Asia takes this advertising technique to extremes. Its ripe fruit can be detected by its smell from half a mile away. Most strangers to the forests in which the durian grows find its smell deeply offensive and when trying to describe it, tend to make comparisons with such things as rotten fish and sewers. Local people however, regard it as one of the greatest of all delicacies and will spend days searching the forests during the right season for a tree in fruit. They have to be quick off the mark, however, for a great number of forest-living animals share the same opinion. Squirrels, hornbills and orang utan collect the fruits while they are still hanging from the tree. Mouse deer, sun bears and even tigers take them when they have fallen. The smell, which attracts them all, comes

from the prickly outer rind. The flesh around the seeds has no smell at all and a taste that bears little connection to that which advertises it. Even strangers who find the durian's smell nauseous may be forced to admit that its taste is delicious.

Within a few days of the fruit becoming ripe, the ground beneath a durian tree is littered with torn rinds and large numbers of the big black seeds that some diners have spat out during their feasts. These, of course, from the tree's point of view, are the failures. They may germinate, but they will not succeed in growing to any height, for they are within the shade of their parent's canopy, and they will not be able to extract much nutriment in ground where their parent's roots are already well established. The successes are those that the eaters of the fruits inadvertently swallowed. They will have been carried away inside stomachs and guts to be ejected, with luck, a considerable distance away. And each, when it falls to the ground, will be accompanied by a dollop of fertiliser to start it on its way.

Not all seeds have to pass through the entire digestive tract in order to be transported. Many birds are able to remove nutritious flesh from around a fruit inside their crop and then regurgitate the seed. This makes considerable sense in those cases where the seeds

◁
An orang utan feasts on a durian in Borneo

A rhinoceros hornbill collecting fruit in the Bornean rain forest
▽

are particularly big for it saves the bird from having to carry around in their stomachs large loads that have no nutritional value. And some of these loads can be very sizable. The stone of a wild avocado is very big indeed, so big in fact that it seems almost impossible that the quetzal bird, which feeds on it, could get it into its beak. But the quetzal's gape is extraordinarily wide for its length and the bird specialises in feeding on this particular fruit. It has exceptionally powerful wing muscles which enable it to beat its wings so rapidly that it can hover in front of a hanging fruit – an extraordinary achievement for a bird almost the size of a crow. It seizes the fruit with its beak, rips it off the branch and swallows it. Then it flies away to a regular perch where eventually, having removed the avocado's soft outer layers within its crop, it regurgitates the stone. The females, it seems, rely on the avocado's extremely nutritious flesh to enable them to produce their eggs. It is so important for them that the birds habitually build their nests close to avocado trees and some say that they cannot breed without a good supply of the fruit.

Passage through an animal's gut is essential for some seeds. The species of acacia whose umbrella shape is so typical of the plains of East Africa encloses its seeds in small twisted pods. These are very rich in protein and many of the plant-eating animals on the plains relish them. Those seeds that remain uneaten on the ground seldom if ever germinate, whereas those that are swallowed with the pods and then pass through an animal's digestive system nearly always do. It used to be thought that this was because stewing in digestive juices weakened the covering of the seeds and made it possible for the infant plant within to break out. The truth, however, is somewhat different. Within a few hours of the acacia tree shedding its pods, large numbers of a particular kind of small beetle fly in, pierce the pods with their sharp ovipositors and lay their eggs within. The eggs hatch rapidly and the tiny grubs then proceed to feed on the acacia's seeds. Unless, that is, the pods are eaten by an animal such as an elephant. Although the elephant grinds up the pods with its teeth, many of the seeds remain unharmed and are swallowed with the mash. In the stomach all the beetle eggs are killed stone dead by the digestive juices. So when the seeds finally return to the outside world with the animal's droppings, they have been freed

◁

A quetzal about to swallow the fruit of a wild avocado. Costa Rica

△
A great Indian rhinoceros takes its evening bathe, beside a plantation of its food plants in a river in Nepal

from their insect pests by the elephant, just as effectively as seeds of wheat that have been treated by a farmer with insecticide.

Some animals drop their dung on special middens. That is likely to be a disadvantage for a seed, which would be better served by a more widespread distribution. But this is not necessarily the case. The great Indian rhinoceros is a creature of regular habits. Each evening it visits one of its regular sites along a river for a wallow. After it has spent some time standing in the cooling water, it emerges on to a mud-bank, where there is plenty of open space around and little danger of it being ambushed by a tiger. And there it defecates.

Now the rhino is a somewhat choosy feeder. It likes particular kinds of grasses. Although it has massive grinding molars, some of the grasses' seeds always escape them and pass out unharmed in the dung. They land on a perfect seed-bed – soft, fine-grained mud, recently deposited by the river and therefore rich in nutrients, but as yet unoccupied by any other seedlings. So the rhino, in effect, plants its own garden with vegetables that match its tastes as precisely as those selected by a keen human gardener for growing in his or her vegetable patch.

One plant in particular benefits from this habit of the rhino – the trewia tree, a kind of euphorbia. Its fruits are large, brown and hard, like small potatoes. They are not covered with soft succulent flesh that might tempt monkeys or birds. They are too big to be swallowed by a small mammal. But the rhino loves them and in consequence it regularly deposits them on the mud banks of rivers. This is exactly what they need, for the young trewia plant will only grow properly in open locations where there is strong light. These days, however, the Indian rhino is becoming rarer and rarer in Nepal. Were it to disappear altogether, then the trewia would lose its courier and ultimately it might no longer line the river banks of southern Nepal as it does today.

More plants than we know about may well have disappeared from the earth because they have lost their contracted transporters. Take, for example, the guanacaste tree of central America. It grows out in open grasslands and produces its seeds enclosed in strange wheel-shaped pods. These are far too big to be carried by the wind. They have no spines with which to attach themselves to animals. They are not coated with succulent flesh that might tempt a bird and they are too large to be swallowed whole by one.

Nonetheless, the rind is full of nutriment, and the seeds inside have hard coats that seem quite tough enough to survive a certain amount of chewing and the digestive acids of a stomach. All this suggests that the guanacaste's courier is likely to be a large grazing animal. And sure enough, the fruits are eagerly eaten by the horses and cows that graze on the plains where it grows. But there is a snag to this explanation. Neither cows nor horses are native to the Americas. They were introduced there from Europe by the Spanish conquistadors four hundred years ago. The form of the guanacaste fruit cannot have changed very much in that short time. So what did it depend on before horses and cattle arrived?

Central America once had a unique and spectacular population of mammals – giant sloths that weighed three tons and could rear up to browse on the branches of trees twenty feet above the ground; huge armadillos with massive domed shells the size of small trucks; and bizarre mammoths. All these creatures were vegetarians and all had both the strength and the teeth to make a meal of guanacaste seeds. It may well have been one or more of these species that over thousands of years became the guanacaste's original courier. There is still a time-gap to be explained, for when the first human beings spread down into central America from the north, about ten thousand years ago, these animals disappeared. They were probably hunted to extinction by the new arrivals. But it seems that human beings also developed a taste for guanacaste seeds. It may have been they who deliberately planted guanacaste seeds out on the plains and so took over the job from the giants they exterminated. Forest-living animals, such as wild pigs and tapirs, on their occasional forays out into open country may also have helped. But it must have been touch and go for the tree for many centuries. And then, in the nick of time, the U.S. cavalry – or rather, the horses of the conquistadors – galloped to its rescue and the guanacaste, once more had reliable, ever-hungry couriers to transport it to new sites on the plains. But it was a close thing.

◇

Encouraging animals to eat seeds is a high-risk strategy from another point of view. The fact that they have been provisioned with food for the young plant makes them very nutritious for animals. In fact they are much more so than either fruit or leaves, so an animal would do well to eat them if it can.

Plants take special steps to prevent this happening. Some fill their seeds with poison. The yew attaches a bright red fleshy covering to its seeds which many birds relish and accordingly transport. Their beaks are not strong enough to damage the seed and that is just as well for it contains a savage poison which can kill bigger animals if they are incautious enough to crush a seed in their mouths. One of the more virulent of plant poisons, strychnine, which human beings extract for their own medicinal or murderous purposes, also comes from a seed.

Very few animals are able to overcome such potentially lethal defences. Macaws, however, have done so. The hura tree protects its explosive fruits with a sap so toxic that it will raise great red welts if it touches human skin and even blind those who get it into their eyes. The macaws, however, are not put off. Long before the fruits are ripe, the birds rip them apart, pods, seeds and all, and then, after a meal that would have poisoned others, they fly to particular places

▷
Macaws assemble on a vine, awaiting their turn to gather anti-indigestion medicine from the clay of a river bank in Peru

on a river bank where they can gnaw out and swallow a special clay which detoxifies their meal.

Armour is a more common defence. None can be more impregnable than that developed by the Brazil nut as many of us, wrestling with one over a Christmas meal, will acknowledge. These nuts are produced inside a large round capsule by the bertholletia tree that grows in the Brazilian rain forest. When it lands with a thump on the forest floor, it nearly always remains intact. To many animals it has little attraction. It has no smell and it is too strong to be cracked. Doubtless, most animals are not even aware that it contains anything edible. But one animal does. The agouti.

This is a rodent the size of a large rabbit that trots nervously through the forest undergrowth on long thin legs. Its front teeth are chisel-sharp and fully capable of cutting through the capsule and the shells of the nuts within to reach the rich flesh they contain. But a single capsule produces twenty or so nuts, far more than an agouti can eat at a single sitting. Rapidly, it gathers them into its cheek pouches. One by one it takes them away, digs a little hole with feverish movements of its delicate front feet, drops the nut in and then covers it up, carefully stamping the earth down afterwards to conceal the site from rivals. Back and forth it hurries until all the nuts have been hidden. Now it will be able to retrieve them at a later date. Happily for the bertholletia tree, however, the agouti's memory is fallible. A considerable proportion of the nuts it hides it never finds again. So by a policy of superabundance – overwhelming its animal courier with more than it can consume at any one time – and at the price of a few nuts being eaten, the tree also succeeds in distributing its large heavy seeds.

The system, however, is less than perfect, for the agouti's range is not great and few of the nuts get carried long distances. A pine tree does a little better. It uses the same strategy of sacrificing a few of its seeds and relying on the forgetfulness of the courier who takes them and conceals them. The pine tree takes two years to construct its seeds. During this long time they are kept safe within hard woody cones, but they are in any case of little interest to animals, for they are not fully formed or very nutritious. But when they are ready, the segments of the cones open and the seeds fall out. Plenty of animals will gather them when they have fallen to the ground,

◁
Brazil nuts being extracted from their capsule by an agouti. Costa Rica

but one bird, the nut-cracker, forestalls other consumers by collecting the seeds just before this happens. It seizes a cone with its foot and hacks it apart with its sharp bill, picking out the seeds one by one.

△
The European nutcracker, a specialised member of the crow family, picks a hazel nut

The bird is just as prudent as the agouti and does its best to cache those it cannot eat immediately. But unlike the agouti, its choice of hiding place is particularly helpful to the pine tree. A nutcracker nearly always buries the seeds in open areas away from shade. That is just the sort of site that suits the seedling and much preferable to one in the shade of other adult pines. And the depth at which the nut-cracker buries the seeds exactly matches the seeds' needs – not so shallow that other hungry animals will easily find them, and not so deep that the seedlings will have difficulty in pushing up through the soil to the light. Fortunately for the pine tree, the nutcracker's memory is no better than the agouti's. Two out of every three seeds the bird buries, it never finds again.

◇

So, one way and another, floating through the sky, drifting over water, entangled in animals' coats and stewing inside their stomachs, many seeds reach destinations where they can start their lives away from the overpowering environmental dominance of their parents. But they do not start on those lives immediately. They await an environmental cue that signals that the time for germination is suitable. In temperate regions where a cold winter is followed by a warm spring, this stimulus may be no more than a rise in temperature. In deserts, it is likely to be a sudden shower of rain. In certain kinds of heathlands, it will be fire. And most seeds are capable of waiting for a considerable time until the moment for them to spring into life is just right.

Desert seeds can remain in the sand for decades, awaiting a shower of rain. One of the longest recorded waits of all is that of a lupin in the Arctic tundra. Its seeds, if they do not get the tiny warming they need in any particular year, may be blown away and swept into crevices in the frozen soil. Decay at these low temperatures

Arctic lupins bloom in the short northern summer. Alaska
▽

proceeds so slowly that dead vegetation accumulates layer upon layer, as peat. If the seeds get buried more deeply than a few inches, they become part of the permafrost, nature's deep-freeze, where nothing melts. Seeds excavated from such layers that are ten thousand years old have been taken to a laboratory and there warmed and watered. A high percentage of them proved to be dead. But a few, miraculously, have come to life.

The Arctic lupin may hold the record for longevity, but there is another example of a return to life which is, perhaps, even more romantic. In 1982, an ancient settlement was being excavated in Japan. It belonged to the Yayoi Period and was estimated to be about two thousand years old. The people who lived there were farmers and stored their harvest in small pits. One was excavated which still contained at the bottom some grains of rice. They were all blackened and dead. But among them lay one seed that was different from all the others. It was taken, planted and watered – and it sprang into life. It was a magnolia.

Its leaves and general form left no doubt in anyone's mind that this was Magnolia kobus, the wild species that is still common today in the surrounding countryside. But then, eleven years later, it produced its first flower bud. As this unfurled, it proved to be different from any other Magnolia kobus alive. That species has six petals. This newly-woken individual had eight. The following year there were over thirty flowers on the tree. The number of petals they carried varied from six to nine. It is too early yet to know whether this variation in the flowers is a temporary aberration or whether it is a true genetically-based character. If it is the latter, then this plant is the sole survivor of an ancient species that disappeared from the face of the earth for a millennium and has remained suspended in limbo, free of all the evolutionary pressures that were modifying its relatives. It, surely, is a sleeping beauty if ever there was one. It is also a marvellous demonstration that plants, in the form of seeds, are not only unexcelled travellers in space, but also incomparable travellers in time.

▷
An ancient Japanese magnolia, after lying dormant for some two thousand years, reveals a strange number of petals

2

FEEDING AND GROWING

T HE SEEDS of a cheese plant are no bigger than orange pips. They develop in spikes of a thousand or so on stems high in the canopy of the central American rain forest, for their parent is a climber. When they ripen and fall, they scatter widely over the forest floor and almost immediately germinate. Green worm-like shoots slowly writhe out of them and begin to extend across the ground, heading for the base of the tree from which they have tumbled. If a great number of them have fallen and they are evenly distributed over the ground, then as the shoots grow they begin to look like the spokes of a huge wheel, the hub of which is the bole of the tree that still supports their parent. It seems almost miraculous that they should all, in some way, know where to go. They do because, like all plants, they can sense the light. But they, unlike most shoots, do not

◁

A young cheese plant begins its ascent of a tree in the South American rain forest, pressing its leaves closely against the bark

▷

Cheese plant seedlings travel across the forest floor towards shade

seek it. They are programmed to avoid it and they head for the nearest deep shade. If their parent was sitting on the far end of a branch, then they may move towards the base of a neighbouring tree. Failing that, they will creep towards the one from which they have fallen. Although they have green skins, they do not produce any food for themselves at this stage. They are fuelled almost entirely from the store their parent bequeathed them in the seed.

If they fail to find a tree trunk within six feet or so, then they run out of fuel and die, exhausted. But if one encounters a vertical surface within that distance, it suddenly changes. Instead of seeking shade, it seeks the light. It begins to climb upwards. Small round leaves spring out from either side of it and they, at last, produce food. With this new fuel supply, it climbs more strongly. As it ascends, its leaves get bigger. By the time it is approaching the canopy, where the light is brighter, its leaves, which are now a foot or so across, begin to divide into segments. In some species, they develop long slits. In one they form the holes reminiscent of Emmenthal cheese that give the plant its popular name. A single cheese plant thus produces three kinds of very differently shaped leaves, each suited to a different circumstance and phase in its life.

Leaves emerge from their buds in many different ways. Those of the cheese plant emerge tightly rolled, like perfectly furled umbrellas. Palms produce theirs neatly packed in pleats. The big fat buds

◁

Nearing the canopy, the cheese plant produces large perforated leaves

▷

A beech leaf breaks free from its bud

of rhubarb push up through the ground and burst to reveal their young leaves squashed and crumpled. Ferns send up their shoots curled in the shape of croziers with each of the side fronds curled in its own crozier-in-miniature. But whatever their style of packing, they all open and spread to their widest extent in order to catch the sunshine as soon as possible.

The crozier of a fern begins to uncoil, revealing leaflets along its sides awaiting their turn

◇

Leaves are the food factories of a plant. The raw materials they use are of the simplest. Carbon dioxide, water and a few mineral ingredients. The first, a gas, is all around them in the air and they absorb it through tiny pores in their surface. Water, and the minerals dissolved in it, is collected by the roots from the ground in which the plant grows. The agents within the tissues of the leaves that process these raw materials are small grains containing that remarkable green substance, chlorophyll. Powered by the energy of the sun, this is able to combine these elements and produce starches and sugars, the foods from which the plant builds its various tissues. The process is called photosynthesis. Its by-product is oxygen. That gas drifts

The pores on the underside of a hyacinth leaf through which the plant breathes
▽

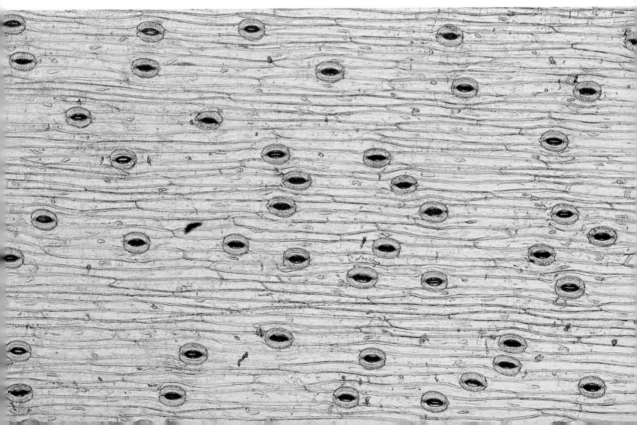

away through the leaf pores into the atmosphere to the benefit of animals. For them it is the very breath of life.

Since daylight is essential for this process, every plant must, as far as possible, position its leaves so that each collects its share without interfering with any others the plant may have. This may require changing the posture of the leaves throughout the day as the sun moves across the sky. The accuracy with which a plant can position them may be judged simply by gazing up at the canopy in a wood. The leaves form a near-continuous ceiling, fitting together like the pieces of a jigsaw.

In an environment where many species live crowded together, as they do in an English hedgerow, plants may have to jockey with their neighbours and rivals for exposure to the sun. Watching them do so on time-lapse film shot over several days is like watching the faces of a packed crowd at a tennis match, where each person is anxious to get a good view of the ball as it passes from one side of

△
Like most woodland trees, the branches of these birches rarely overlap one another but form an interlocking mosaic in the near-continuous canopy

the court to the other. In the morning, they face eastwards. As the sun rises, so they crane upwards; and as it sets, so they turn westwards. Overnight, some may fold up, but all realign themselves to be ready to face the sun when it appears once more at dawn in the east.

On the floor of a well-established forest, the light may be very dim indeed. Some plants deal with the problem by growing extremely large leaves. The biggest undivided leaf of all belongs to a giant edible aroid that grows in marshy parts of the tropical rain forest in Borneo. One of its heart-shaped leaves may be ten feet across and have a surface area of over thirty square feet. Other members of the same family do not grow such monstrous leaves but maximise the meagre light that falls on them in a different way. They coat the underside of their leaves with a purple pigment. This catches the light after it has passed through the thickness of the leaf and reflects it back into the leaf tissues so that the chlorophyll has

The largest of all undivided leaves, those of a giant member of the arum family in south-east Asia
▽

a second chance to utilise what is left of it. Begonias, which also grow on the floor of these Asiatic forests, have an additional trick. Some cells in the upper surface of their leaves are transparent and act as tiny lenses, gathering the feeble light and focussing it on to the grains of chlorophyll within.

The second essential, water, is sucked in by the tiny hairs and rootlets that grow from a plant's roots. It is piped up to the leaves through tubes in the stem or trunk and along the veins that run through the stalks and into every part of the leaves. If the soil is rich, the water will carry dissolved in it the minerals and other nutrients that are necessary for constructing particular parts of the plant's body.

To find water, a plant has to position its roots with just as much precision as it arranges its leaves. If moisture is in very short supply, then a plant may have to drive a tap root deep into the ground to reach the water table. Some desert plants have had to develop root systems that are far deeper than they are tall and extend laterally a very long way beyond the furthest extent of their foliage. Even if

△
Leaves on the forest floor make most of the meagre light. Herringbone plants (left above and below) from South America and a begonia (right above) do so with pigment-free areas on their upper surface; another begonia (right below) has a red-pigmented underside which reflects light passing through the thickness of the leaf into its interior

▷
The roots of a tree in the tropical Pacific extend both laterally and deeply in their search for water

the environment is well-watered, a plant may still need to compete with others for this essential commodity, so it positions a network of roots within a few inches of the soil surface, where it can gather the rain water before others can. That is also the best place to claim the soluble nutrients released by decay from the fallen leaves and other vegetable detritus that lies on the surface of the ground.

With abundant supplies of water and nutrients, and in good light, plants can become very large. Competing with their neighbours for sunlight leads them to grow taller, but if they are to do that, they have to have structures that will prevent them from toppling over. Roots become thicker and spread through the surface layers of the soil to form a broad support platform. A few may provide additional anchorage by plunging vertically downwards. In places where such deep roots cannot develop, perhaps because the soil is no more than a shallow layer over solid rock, or because it contains so much sticky clay that oxygen cannot permeate through it, a tree may thicken some of its lateral roots so extremely that they form immense buttresses that snake across the forest floor.

To grow tall, plants must have a rigid stem. That rigidity is produced by depositing within the core of the stem a hard, strong substance called lignin. The cells in which it is laid down now cease to be living elements that can transport liquids. They have become dead tissue – timber. From now on, their function is simply to stiffen and support the plant's body. With such strengthening, plants become very large indeed.

◇

◁

Mountain ash eucalypts in south-eastern Australia grow to a height of over 300 feet. Below, forming an understorey, tree-ferns fifteen feet high spread their wide crowns

The tallest of all flowering plants is the Australian mountain ash. British colonialists, settling in lands far away from Europe, had a cheerful disregard for any kind of biological accuracy when it came to bestowing names on the animals and plants they encountered in their new homes. They simply gave them the name of the European animal or plant to which they had some superficial resemblance. If a bird had a red breast they called it a robin even though it was a flycatcher. And the gigantic, noble tree that formed great forests in the hills of the newly founded states of Victoria and Tasmania, they called an ash even though it is obviously a member of that wide-spread, abundant and typically Australian family, the eucalypts.

The mountain ash's scientific name is Eucalyptus regnans which means, accurately enough, the ruling eucalypt. That indeed would certainly be a much better English name for such a magnificent giant. Walking through a forest of them it is difficult to appreciate just how gigantic they are, for the relative proportions of their trunks and branches are very much like those of smaller eucalypt species. In fact they stand over three hundred feet high. The current record holder is said to be one in the Styx Valley of Tasmania which has been measured as reaching 325 feet. Even this is not the tallest that has ever existed. The forests of Australia, like those almost everywhere else, have been plundered for timber ever since Europeans first entered them. Back in 1880, a surveyor measured a mountain ash in Victoria that stood 375 feet high. It was, of course, immediately cut down. Around the same time, an official inspector of forests reported a fallen trunk of one that was 435 feet long. That may well be the tallest tree ever measured.

On a hot day, a tree the size of a mountain ash can lose several hundred gallons of water as vapour from its leaves. If those leaves are not to wilt, that water has to be continuously replaced. The tree has to gather it with its roots, raise it several hundred feet in its trunk and send it along its branches and stalks into the leaves themselves. A fireman, perched on top of his tallest ladder, can only get water into his hose if it is pumped up by a huge vibrating engine roaring away on the ground beneath. Yet a tree manages to do a similar thing with no visible movement and in total silence. How?

It is only able to do so because the tensile strength of water is very great indeed; that is to say, an enclosed column of it will not break into separate droplets except under enormous tension. The vessels up which the water travels were initially formed by extremely elongated cells. As they grew, these not only thickened their sides with lignin but ultimately broke down the dividing wall where they met, tip to tip, so that together they formed long continuous tubes uninterrupted by any divisions. That done, the cells died. The pipes they created are thus inert and dead. They are also full of water. As the cells in a leaf lose water by evaporation, so it is replaced by water from the top of the tubes and the whole water column is pulled upwards. This, of course puts a huge strain on the sides of the tubes within a tall tree, but their woody walls are rigid enough to withstand it, and the tensile strength of water normally prevents it from fragmenting. Under extreme conditions the system breaks down. But it is not the tree's vessels that collapse; it is the water column that breaks. If, during droughts, you put a stethoscope to a badly-stressed tree, you can hear the clicks from within as this happens.

The function of leaves is not to absorb water. Indeed, if water lies on them for too long, it will interfere with the process of gas exchange. Many leaves, therefore, have shapes and structures that help to get rid of it. Hairs on their surface gather water into droplets around them, so keeping it away from the pores. Grooves channel

▷
In the rain forest, water is channelled from the surface of a leaf by way of its drip-tip. Borneo

the water across the leaf's surface. Spiky tips at the end of a leaf help it to drain off.

All these features make good functional sense. Even so there is still some mystery about the shapes of leaves. How is it that closely related plants, often growing side by side, may have leaf differences that enable us to identify them as two separate species? When such specific differences occur between two closely related birds, such as, for example, a chaffinch and a greenfinch, ornithologists will explain that such markings have evolved as indicators that enable a courting bird to identify another as belonging to the same species and therefore a potential mate. But that explanation cannot apply to, for example, an English elm and a wych elm. Both are native to southern England and may stand side by side. Plants do not actively choose their mates or need to recognise their appearance. So why should the English elm's leaf be rounder with a longer stalk than a wych elm's? No one knows. On the other hand, there are families of trees, such as the dipterocarps which dominate the rain forests of south-east Asia, whose multitude of very different species have leaves that are so similar that it is virtually impossible to distinguish between them.

◇

The sugars and starches that plants manufacture in their leaves as food for themselves can, of course, serve equally well as food for animals. Indeed, all animals depend ultimately on such vegetarian foods. Many do so directly. Others do so at second hand because they eat the flesh of animals that fed on plants. So every plant, everywhere, is potentially under the threat of attack by animals. The most widespread and often the least visible of these depredations are made by insects. Day and night in a summer woodland, uncountable billions of insect jaws are destroying the plants' precious leaves. Bugs and aphids plunge their needle-like mouthparts into the veins and suck the sap. Caterpillars nibble their way through leaves and bore into buds. Some perch on the margins of leaves and chew their way inwards, occasionally working in such hordes that the afflicted plant is totally stripped. Others feed more secretively,

▷
Caterpillars feeding on a leaf

△
A spray of leaves from an Australian bottle-brush damaged by sawfly caterpillars

tunnelling their way into the substance of a leaf and then munching through the soft succulent cells of the leaf's interior. Their activities become visible on the surface of the leaf as an irregular blotch, a winding track, or a scroll of such geometric perfection and regularity that it looks like the decorative flourish of a skilled calligrapher.

In the rain forests of Borneo, one small moth caterpillar constructs a most ingenious device that enables it to feed out of the sight of hungry birds. It starts work on the margin of a leaf and chews a cut inwards as though it were about to remove a semicircular segment. But when it reaches the farthest extent of the curve and seems about to arch back towards the margin, it stops and returns to the edge of the leaf. It walks along it and makes another cut as if to complete the semicircle from the other direction. But just before it joins the first cut, it stops. The segment is now attached only by a small hinge.

The caterpillar next spins silken threads across the hinge between the segment and the rest of the leaf. As the silk dries, it contracts. This first hoists the segment into the air and then brings it down on top of the caterpillar. Now, working from beneath, the caterpillar makes a short slit at right angles to the cut edge of the segment. It pulls one edge of this across the other so creating a pleat. This converts the segment into a tiny dome. The whole process takes a couple of hours. As a result of all this ingenious labour, the

▷
A leaf-folding caterpillar makes a safe dining-room for itself where it can eat out of the sight of hungry birds

caterpillar can nibble away at the leaf surface beneath, safe from the eyes and beaks of hungry birds.

Other caterpillars build shelters for themselves that, in comparison with the Bornean caterpillar's tiny wigwam, are giant marquees. A European moth that is a serious pest in orchards, lays its eggs in spirals glued together around the twigs of fruit trees. When they hatch, the young caterpillars, while sustaining themselves by eating the leaves immediately around them, spin a large silken shroud around the branch so big that it can accommodate them all. They spend the day within it, concealed from the sight of hungry predatory birds. But when night comes they set out in long columns to demolish more leaves.

After they have eaten everything in their immediate neighbourhood, a single scout sets out to prospect for more. As it explores new parts of the tree, it lays down behind it a trail of scent that exudes from glands on its rear end. This enables it to find its way back to shelter before dawn. The next night, its companions inspect the trail. If it has a single track, as might happen if the caterpillar was taken in the night by some hunter, they will ignore it. But if there is a double track, indicating that the scout returned and if, furthermore, its smell indicates that the scout had a good meal, then the whole colony of several hundred will set off in procession to strip the leaves from yet another part of the fruit tree.

The surfaces of leaves and the walls of the cells within them are made, like the rest of a plant's structures, of cellulose. Unlike the sap and the soluble foods dissolved in it, cellulose is extremely indigestible. It passes through the guts of plundering insects virtually unchanged. Nor are bigger animals any better at digesting it. Those that have become specialist leaf-feeders can only extract nourishment from it by enlisting the aid of a very different kind of living organism – bacteria. They, unlike any animal, can digest cellulose.

Rabbits maintain such bacterial colonies in their stomachs but even so need to process their meals twice. Having eaten their fill of vegetation by the evening, they retreat to their burrows and there during the night they excrete the partially digested remains as mucus-covered pellets. These the rabbit picks up in its mouth and swallows once more, so as to extract the rest of the nourishment they contain.

▷
A brood of North American tent-making caterpillars build a silken marquee for themselves

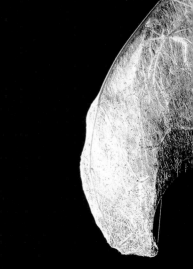

Cows and other ruminants provide their bacterial colonies with special compartments of the stomach. Leaves, having been chewed and swallowed, are given an initial processing by the bacteria, and then sent back up to the mouth to be given a second mastication, before they are swallowed yet again and digested in the main part of the stomach.

Leaf-eating monkeys have to face the same problem. The colobus monkey of Africa and the leaf monkey of India also have large chambered stomachs but perhaps the most spectacularly bellied monkey of all is the proboscis monkey of Borneo. Families of them feed together in the morning for several hours, largely on the leaves of mangroves, selecting the newly-sprouted ones with great care. In the afternoon they then take extended siestas to allow their bacteria to deal with the consequences.

◇

In spite of the drawbacks of cellulose, leaves remain a very tempting food for a great range of animals large and small. Plants, accordingly, have gone to considerable lengths in order to protect themselves and minimise this damaging robbery. Animals, in response, have had to develop ways of circumventing these defences in order to feed. So, over the long history of evolution, there has been an ever-escalating arms-war between animals and plants.

Big browsing animals can be deflected, to some extent, by spikes and thorns. Holly does so modestly with prickles on its leaves. Hawthorn sprouts spikes on its twigs. In tropical forests, palms and rattan arm themselves to a spectacular degree with needles that can be a foot long. On the plains of east Africa, acacias defend themselves in similar way. The thorns grown by the buffalo acacia are so long, so sharp and bristle in such numbers that human beings can scarcely push one of their branches out of the way without getting badly scratched. Yet giraffe and camels and goats have developed tongues that are so long, mobile and dexterous that they can select and grasp any particular shoot that they want, and the linings to their mouths seem to be so leathery that they can close around the thorns without damage of any kind.

◁

A male proboscis monkey in a Bornean swamp makes a meal of mangrove leaves

△
A giraffe, deterred by neither height nor a battery of thorns, tackles an acacia

The varying success of browsers influences the shape and the future of the acacias. While they are still small and animals can reach every part of them, they form low rounded bushes. But if they are well nourished and successful, they may grow so large that antelope browsing the periphery cannot reach the topmost twigs in the centre. Free of attack, these now sprout rapidly upwards forming a central tower. Only if that happens does the acacia have the chance of becoming a full grown tree. As its trunk thickens, its energies are diverted from the lower branches and they gradually disappear as the tree grows up beyond the reach of most animals other than giraffe.

◁
An African acacia escapes from life as a bush to become a tree

The defences developed by grasses become only too clear if you carelessly run your finger along the blade of one of the coarser meadow grasses. You may well cut yourself. The damage is done by a line of microscopic silica blades. Grasses must have developed the ability to incorporate silica in their tissues very early in the interaction between them and the animals that seek to graze them, for the animals have themselves evolved a major anatomical change in response. The roots of their teeth do not close when they are

◁
*The silica blades
set in the edge of a
leaf of grass*

adult, as happens in other mammals, but instead remain open
throughout their lives and so are able to grow continuously. As the
particles of silica in the grass wear down the tops of their teeth, new
growth at the roots in the jaw pushes the teeth upwards to compensate.

Other plants defend themselves even more aggressively. They
sting. The nettle's sting is a modified hair. Its tip is a minute glassy

◁
*The poisoned
hypodermic
needles of a nettle*

△
A female red admiral butterfly selects nettle leaves on which to lay her eggs so that her young, when they hatch, will find food that few other insects will tackle

needle which if given even the slightest touch, breaks off. The broken edges are so sharp that they can cut skin. At the same time a poison held in a small chamber at the bottom of the hair squirts into the wound. The poison causes us considerable pain. And not only us. Those indefatigable nibblers, rabbits, have sensitive noses and also find the sting very unpleasant, and they too leave nettles strictly alone. Smaller creatures however, can feed more fastidiously. The caterpillars of small tortoiseshell and red admiral butterflies chew their way around the dangerous needles and the succulent leaves of nettles, so shunned by other bigger animals, are one of their favourite foods.

There are even more ferocious stingers elsewhere in the world. Tropical Australia has three different species. Some are low bushes. One is a tree that can grow to fifty feet tall. A traveller failing to

recognise the large and characteristic heart-shaped leaves and brushing past them is likely to be so badly stung that he may have to be taken to hospital. The poison, like that of the nettle, contains histamine but also other as yet unidentified venoms that cause an intense pain which can last for weeks. There is no known antidote.

Just as there are bogus animal warriors who boast with vivid warning colours of weapons that they do not possess, so there are harmless plants that mimic the appearance of well-armed species and so save the expense of developing weapons. The deadnettle and its relative the yellow archangel have leaves which resemble those of the stinging nettle. The imitation is so close that few animals will risk a nibble of either. Yet both are harmless.

Mimicry is used in a more devious way by the passion vine of central and South America. The caterpillars of the black, yellow and red heliconius butterfly feed upon its leaves. An adult female

△
The unarmed leaves of the yellow archangel (right) resemble those of the stinging nettle (left) so closely that many animals avoid both

always lays her eggs on this particular vine so that her offspring, when they hatch, will have food immediately in front of them. But if she finds eggs like hers already deposited on the vine, she will lay elsewhere, for there may not be enough food for two broods of caterpillars. The vine has exploited this habit. It produces small yellow knobs, in one species at the base of many of its leaves, in another on their undersides, that closely mimic the appearance of heliconius eggs. A female, seeing them, moves away to lay elsewhere. But why should not the passion vine decorate its leaves with so many egg replicas that the butterflies are totally deterred? Perhaps if it did the butterflies, in response, would develop the ability to distinguish between the real and the imitation. One thing is certain – evolution is a continuing process and it cannot be assumed that all these conflicts have necessarily reached a stalemate. The subtle battle between the butterfly and the passion vine is doubtless still continuing.

It is difficult for a plant to avoid attack by hiding its leaves, for leaves, in order to fulfil their function, must stretch out to catch the light and in doing so, necessarily make themselves conspicuous. Yet

The rounded shape of the pebble plant's leaves not only minimise loss of moisture but make it difficult to recognise among the gravels of the Kalahari Desert
▽

one or two plants, most ingeniously, have overcome this fundamental difficulty. Pebble plants live in the deserts of Africa. They are only a few inches across and grow close to the ground within easy range of any browser. They have only two stumpy leaves, but these leaves are bloated with liquid, and that must make them very desirable to animals living in this arid environment. Yet the pebble plant is rarely if ever attacked for its leaves are mottled in colours that exactly match the stones among which it grows. Thirsty grazers simply don't see it.

Sensitive mimosa manages to conceal its leaves in a way that is, literally, electrifying. It is common throughout the tropics, sprawling across the ground in clearings and along roadsides. Its leaves are feathery, with rows of small leaflets rising from either side of its stems. Spread out in the sunshine, they must look delicious to any hungry leaf-eating insect. But when a grasshopper or a locust lands on them, the leaflets suddenly disappear. Within seconds, they fold upwards to lie tight alongside the stem so that what was obviously luxuriant foliage is suddenly reduced to nothing more than a tangle of unappetising twigs. If in spite of this the insect does not lose interest and starts to bite the plant, the leaves make a second movement, downwards, which exposes the sharp barbs on the stems. The grasshopper, baffled, hops away.

▷

The sensitive plant folds away its leaflets within three seconds of being touched

The mechanism that brings about this transformation is triggered by minute electric currents, similar to those that pass along our own nerves. The plant does not have such special power-lines to carry the current and consequently its reactions are not nearly as fast as ours. Nonetheless the signal, transmitted along the ducts that carry its sap, can travel the whole length of a foot-long stem within a second or so. The warmer the temperature, the quicker the reaction will be. The base of each leaflet, where it joins the stem, is greatly swollen. The cells within are turgid, filled tight with liquid. When the signal arrives, those in the lower half of the swelling immediately discharge their water which is equally swiftly taken up by those in the upper half. And the leaf collapses downwards. So as the signal travels along the stem, the leaflets fold up one after the other like a line of falling dominoes. After such a defensive collapse, the plant takes about twenty minutes to pump up its cells again and

reopen its leaflets to the sunshine so that they can resume their work of food production.

The most widespread of all methods of leaf protection is neither physical nor mechanical, but chemical. Plants manufacture substances that, in one way or another, deter their attackers. Some of their techniques are astonishingly sophisticated. A wild species of South American potato discharges a message-chemical, a pheromone, which resembles that emitted by aphids when they are under attack. So those aphids never land on it. An African bugleweed synthesises in its tissues a substance similar to the hormone that controls the development of caterpillars. If a caterpillar is persuaded, experimentally, to ingest that substance, then when it turns into a butterfly it will develop two heads and die. Those caterpillars in the wild not surprisingly avoid the bugleweed.

Many plants, however, use a quite straightforward chemical defence. Poison. Bracken, that most widespread of ferns in Britain, fills its young tender leaves with cyanide. That deters most insects. Only a few, such as the caterpillars of the sawfly and the buff ermine moth, are able to tolerate it. By the time the leaves are mature and so tough that they seem likely to be of interest only to larger grazers such as rabbits and deer, they have manufactured a cocktail of toxins so powerful that they can cause blindness and cancer in mammals. Thanks to this, and an ability to spread by proliferating underground stems, bracken is able to dominate huge areas of hillside.

The African acacias, well-protected though they may be by their thorns, use distasteful chemicals in their leaves as a second line of defence. Furthermore, and most remarkably, they warn one another that they are doing so. At the same time as they fill their leaves with poison, they release ethylene gas which drifts out of the pores of their leaves. Other acacias within fifty yards are able to detect this gas and as soon as they do so, they themselves begin to manufacture poison and distribute it to their leaves. A browsing animal soon finds that the tree it first attacked is no longer fit to eat and moves away. But it has to go some distance, for the rest of the acacias nearby have been forewarned – and are now fore-armed.

Milkweed gets its name from a poisonous latex that exudes from its broken stem. This is so toxic that it can give a small animal a

△
A monarch caterpillar demolishes a milkweed's shoot

heart attack. The monarch butterfly, however, has developed an immunity to it. Its caterpillars nibble away at the leaves with impunity. But they do not digest the poison. Instead, they appropriate it and use it for their own purposes. In some way they are able to separate the toxin in the latex and store it unaltered in their bodies. This not only prevents them from succumbing to it, but makes them poisonous to any predator that might swallow them. To make sure that they are not attacked, they advertise the fact that they are unpalatable by being brilliantly coloured. And this is not the end of the story. When the caterpillar turns into a butterfly, it carries the poison with it into its new incarnation. So the butterfly too becomes unpalatable and it too is so brightly and conspicuously coloured that most insect-feeding birds which regularly attack butterflies leave the monarch butterfly strictly alone. Nor has this evolutionary conflict yet reached a conclusion. Black-backed orioles in northern Mexico, unlike most other birds, have now discovered that the butterflies store the poison in their skins and wings. When they catch one they carefully discard these parts, and dine quite happily on the rest.

The ability to produce poison may be the cause of one of the most celebrated, almost mythic, events in natural history – the mass suicide of the Norway lemming. These little hamster-like rodents of the Arctic tundra increase in numbers year after year until there is a population explosion, and then hordes of them are said to deliberately drown themselves.

The cause of this extraordinary behaviour may be the fact, recently discovered, that when lemmings start to feed on the cotton grass and sedges that are their main food, the plants begin to produce a poison which neutralises the lemmings' digestive juices. If the grazing is light, the plants stop doing this after about 30 hours, but if it is intense, as it is when the lemming population reaches its climax, then they do so continuously. The effect on the lemmings is not only that they cannot digest their meals. Because they cannot, their bodies produce more and more digestive fluids, draining their physical resources and bringing them even closer to starvation. As a consequence, the more they eat the hungrier they get, and when having stripped the surrounding tundra they reach the edge of the sea or a lake, they swim out into it, in a frenzied attempt to find some food somewhere that will sustain them.

◇

While it is true that all animals have to turn ultimately to plants for their food, there are one or two instances where the situation is reversed. In some particularly impoverished environments – bogs, moorlands, mountain slopes washed by heavy rains – plants, to survive, have to feed on animals.

The simplest feeder among these vegetable carnivores is the marsh pitcher. Its scientific name is Heliamphora. A belief that the first part of this word means not 'marsh', as it does, but 'sun' has

▷
The marsh pitcher, the simplest of the pitcher plants, traps insects in its curled water-filled leaves

led to it being referred to popularly as a 'sun pitcher'. That is not only a faulty translation but an extremely inappropriate one for it quite misrepresents the plant and does no justice to the problems it faces. The marsh pitchers grow only on the flat summits of a number of isolated sandstone plateaus in south-eastern Venezuela which for much of the time are swathed in cloud and drenched by rain. Five different species have been discovered, each inhabiting its own individual plateau. They spend very little of their lives in sunshine. In this bleak environment, where there is little or no soil and the processes of decay which elsewhere release nutriment from vegetable debris, proceed only very slowly, many plants have to supplement their diet with the bodies of insects.

The marsh pitcher's trap is a very simple one. Its foot-long leaves are curled lengthwise and joined at the margin to form a tall vertical tube. At the top, the tip of the midrib flares into a reddish-rimmed hood that carries a great number of nectar-producing glands. The abundant rains keep these trumpets filled with water. If they were topped up to the very brim, they might be so heavy that they would be in danger of bursting, or at any rate, toppling over. But this does not happen. The seam joining the margins of the leaf is not fastened along its entire length. It stops an inch or so below the upper rim and the resultant vertical slit acts as a safety overflow. One species has a ring of small holes encircling the tube a little below the upper margin and these too act as overflows if the water level gets too high.

Flies and mosquitoes, attracted by the sweet fragrance of the nectar, alight on the hood. As they explore the plant in search of more nectar, they tend to move down into the tube. But this is covered with long, slippery, downward-pointing hairs. Losing their grip, the insects slip downwards. That worsens their situation, for they descend to a section of the tube where the walls have no hairs at all but are smooth and waxy. Down they slide until they tumble into the water. Unable to get any purchase on the surrounding walls, they drown. Bacterial decay then dissolves the tiny corpses and the marsh pitcher absorbs the resulting soup.

In the southern part of the United States, another member of the same family, the trumpet pitcher, has elaborated this simple structure. The hood at the top is much bigger and so vividly coloured

▷
The trumpet pitcher's conspicuous yellow discs are not flowers but lures to attract insects into the traps below. The true flowers are the smaller globular structures

These trumpet
pitchers have been
sectioned to show
the ants and bugs
they have captured

that it might be mistaken at first sight for a flower. One species is
purple, another a glorious gold, and yet another is white veined
with red. Nectar glands cover these hoods so densely that they
glisten. Additional glands are scattered rather more thinly all over
the outer surface of the trumpet itself. And the liquid within is more
potent than the Venezuelan marsh pitchers, for it is quite capable
by itself of digesting insects without any help from bacteria.

There are eight species of trumpet pitcher. One, the huntsman's
cup, has trumpets which start lying on the ground and then curve
upwards, rather like a hunting horn. The biggest, the yellow trumpet, holds its traps vertically upright and stands over three feet high.

△

Almost hidden below the lip of a trumpet pitcher, a small frog lurks ready to collect any insect that the plant attracts

A small green frog sometimes sits within the throat of this species, clearly waiting for insects that are attracted by the plant's nectar and hoping to snap them up before the trumpet pitcher has a chance to drown them. But there are reports that the frog may pay for its daring. On occasion, one retreats too far down the trumpet's throat and enters the smooth-walled sector. Unable to keep its foothold, it tumbles into the digestive bath at the bottom and there succumbs. A meal like that must presumably sustain a trumpet pitcher for years.

The most elaborate of all these leaves turned into pit-fall traps are developed by the plants that are known, simply and without qualification, as pitcher plants. There are over sixty different species of them. Their headquarters are in South-east Asia, but they extend as far west as Madagascar and as far east as Australia. The process of pitcher formation starts when the tip of a leaf begins to extend into a tendril. This gains support for itself by twisting around the stem of another plant, usually making no more than a single turn. Its tip begins to swell and to droop under its own weight. Then, quite suddenly, it inflates with air. As it balloons larger and larger, flecks of colour appear in its walls. Now it begins to fill with fluid. When its growth is complete, a lid-like segment at the top opens. The trap is now ready to receive visitors.

The shape of these pitchers varies with the species. There are beakers and flagons, narrow-necked claret decanters and tall thin champagne flutes. Small ones hang like unlit lamps along the branches of a supporting tree. The biggest of all, the rajah pitcher, sits squatly on the ground. Its huge big-bellied foot-long ponds can easily hold as much as four pints of fluid. Some are said to contain as much as seven.

Their trapping strategy is the same as the trumpet pitchers. They entice insects with fragrant nectar. The walls of their traps are made even more treacherous by a flaky waxy surface that peels off and clogs the feet of insects so that they lose all chance of adhesion. As their victims tumble into the water and start to struggle to save themselves, the disturbance stimulates glands in the pitcher walls which start to discharge a digestive acid. This is so powerful that a fly will be reduced to a hollow shell within days and a midge will disappear entirely within hours. The whole device is so effective that these pitchers can trap not just small insects, but cockroaches, centipedes and scorpions. The rajah is said to be able to consume mice.

These pitchers also have their lodgers. The larvae of various insects have developed an immunity to the pitchers' digestive fluids and feed on the detritus, vegetable as well as animal, that accumulates in the bottom of the pitcher. Other larvae hang in the upper levels, occasionally swooping down to seize one of the detritus feeders. The pitcher may well derive some benefit from having a few such privileged lodgers. As they breathe, so like all animals, they give off carbon dioxide and that, of course, the pitcher needs for its food production. The lodgers' excrement, rich in nitrogen, drifts down to the bottom, and that too is valuable nutriment for the plant. The lodgers also chew up remains of corpses that the pitcher finds indigestible. This prevents big fragments from settling on to the bottom of the pitcher and starting to decay, so rotting the pitcher wall.

The twin-spurred pitcher has made special provision for such companions. In one part of its stem it develops a small chamber that is used as a home by ants. They regularly dive into the liquid, haul

▷

The tendril of a pitcher plant, over a period of two to three weeks inflates to form a liquid-filled trap

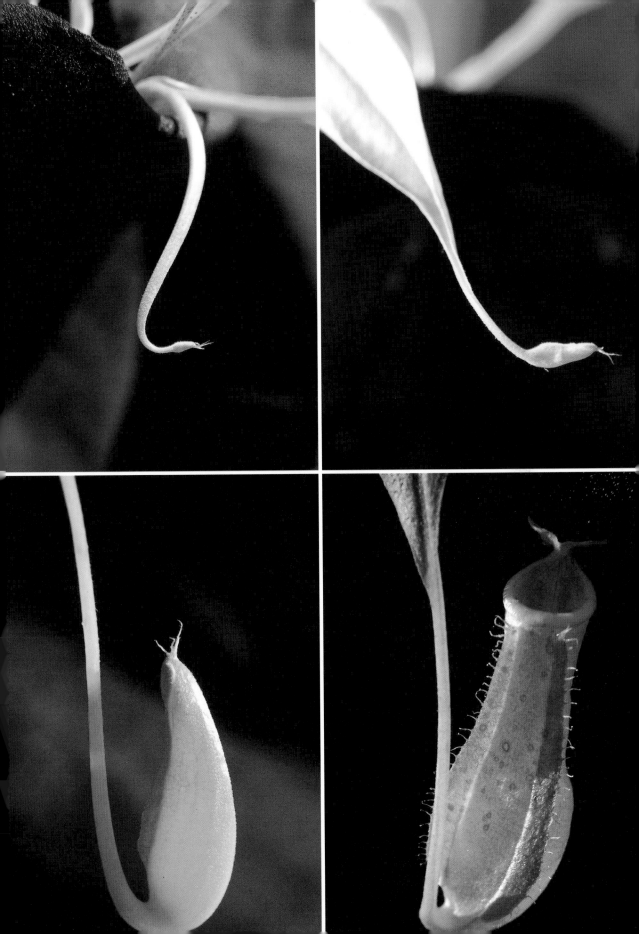

▷

*An ample meal of
insects collected by
a Javanese pitcher
plant*

◁

*Pitcher plants'
traps vary
according to both
the species and
where they develop
on an individual
plant. The phial
pitcher (top left)
has globular traps
only two inches
across whereas
those of Raffles'
pitcher (top right)
are a foot deep:
Low's pitcher
(bottom left) is a
climber and dangles
its traps in the air,
whereas the hairy
pitcher (bottom
right) usually rests
its six-inch traps on
the ground*

dead insects on to the lip and there butcher them. Some of the pieces they take away for their own consumption but others drop back into the pool and are there more easily digested by the plant in this fragmentary form than they would be otherwise. The phial pitcher has perhaps the biggest regular lodger of all – a half-inch long crab with a red belly and claws and a back mottled with black and olive. No more than one of these crabs has ever been found in any one pitcher, but what it takes from the pitcher and whether it gives anything in return has yet to be discovered.

◇

Leaves converted into pitchers and trumpets, efficient though they may be at catching insects, are passive devices. A few leaves, how-ever, have been turned into active traps. Sundews grow in European bogs and marshes. Three-quarters of the family live in western Australia. There they are also found in well-drained woodlands and heaths where the soil is also extremely poor in nutrients. Although some are scramblers or even climbers, many are rosette plants about

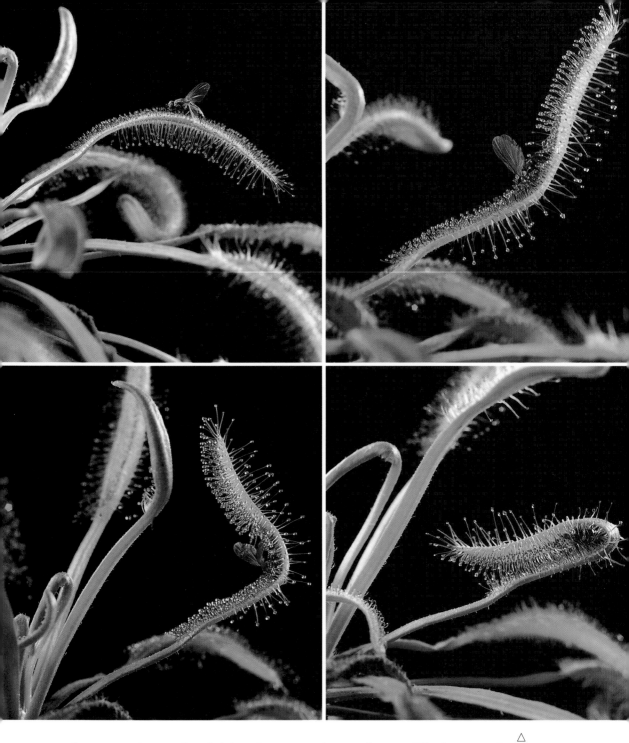

the same size as the daisies that grow in our lawns. The leaves of all are covered with hairs that on the outer margins may be half an inch long. Each of them, provided that the weather is not too dry, carries on its tip a glistening sticky bead. The whole leaf looks to our eyes as entrancing as a bauble of Venetian glass. Insects too must find them attractive, for in spite of the fact that these leaves

△
A South African sundew secures a fly with sticky hairs. Then, over a period of hours, the whole leaf bends to enfold the fly, so hastening its digestion

carry no enticements of nectar, insects are drawn to them. When one alights, it inevitably sticks to a hair. As it struggles, it touches other hairs and becomes further entangled. Neighbouring hairs, even if they have not been touched, are able to sense that a catch has been made and they bend towards it. If the insect is a large one and has been caught near the edge of the leaf, the hairs will lean over and convey the captive towards the centre. There, a whole group of hairs arch over it. The glistening beads contain not only glue but a digestive fluid that soon begins to dissolve the insect's body. The hairs then start to absorb their victim's substance. If the captured insect is particularly large, the whole leaf may fold to enclose it and complete the process.

▷
A crane-fly, caught initially by its wing, is unable to escape as the sundew bends to strengthen its hold

These movements of the hairs are achieved by a swift differential growth of the cells of one side. Once initiated, this proceeds at an extraordinary speed. An outward pointing hair can turn through 180 degrees to point inwards in less than a minute. Because the sundew's movements are produced by growth in the length of hairs, it cannot be repeated indefinitely. Three times seems to be the maximum. But when one walks over a carpet of sundews that spreads over many a bog, the wonder is not whether each leaf has the ability to make a fourth catch, but how even a small proportion of the plants can find enough insects to sustain themselves. Indeed, recent

△
*A fly is attracted
by the glistening
surface of a leaf of
Venus' flytrap and
advances towards
a trigger-hair*

research has shown that although the captures made by the leaves are certainly very valuable, the plant must still draw most of its nitrogen from the soil

There can be no question, however, as to the most spectacular of all these hunting plants. It is, surely, Venus's flytrap. This is related to the sundews, but it is the only species of that family to have evolved such an elaborate trap and it lives only in one small patch of marshy coastal country straddling the border between North and South Carolina. It too is a rosette a few inches across. It has narrow green leaves that at the end are prolonged into two reddish, kidney-shaped lobes on either side of the midrib. The outer margin of each lobe is fringed by a line of spikes and, just beneath them, there is a band of nectar glands. The open face of each lobe carries a few isolated bristly hairs. There are usually three, but there may be two, four or, just occasionally, more.

An insect, attracted by the nectar or the red coloration can crawl around on the surface of a lobe with impunity, provided it doesn't touch one of these bristles, for they are triggers. Even touching one is not necessarily lethal, for nothing will happen immediately. But if it touches the same one or another on the leaf within twenty

△
*The two halves of
the flytrap's leaves
snap together and
the fly is caught*

seconds, then – with a swiftness that may alarm a watching botanist, accustomed as he is to more sedate reactions from his subjects – the two lobes snap together. The reaction takes no more than a third of a second. The stimulus that triggers it is an electric one, like that of the sensitive mimosa, but exactly what mechanism drives the closure is, even now, not fully understood.

Although the trap has been sprung, the insect, if it is small, can escape. The spikes on the leaf margins interlock neatly, but not very tightly. A mosquito or an ant can easily crawl out between them. But for larger insects such as a fly, there is no escape. As it thrashes about in its prison, it inevitably touches the triggers again. This stimulates the cells within the lobes to increase rapidly in number, as happens in the bending hairs of a sundew, and the two segments press closer together. They do so with such firmness that the bulge of a fly's body may become visible on the outside. The edges of the lobes form a hermetic seal and within, digestive solutions rich in hydrochloric acid pour from glands on the face of the lobes and start to dissolve the fly's body.

There are two moments during this process when the plant may seem to be less than efficient as a trapper, but both can be interpreted as safety measures that prevent the trap being sprung unnecessarily or uneconomically. Why should the plant require its victim to touch a trigger hair twice in quick succession? In order that the leaf is not made to close by a inanimate object such as a blown leaf falling on to it. And why are the marginal spikes not set closer together? Because an insect below a certain size will not provide enough sustenance to compensate for the energy spent in digesting it. If the insect is so small that it does escape, then after twenty minutes or so, the two lobes begin to reopen and twenty four hours later they are all set to try again.

◇

So leaves, one way or another, produce all the foods a plant needs for growth. The methods used by the vast majority of them to do this require that they should be flat in order to capture sunshine, and thin to allow gases and water vapour to diffuse freely throughout them. In tropical rain forests, where there is abundant moisture and warmth, such a shape presents no problems. But in other parts of the world, where it is much dryer or much colder, that shape makes leaves very vulnerable.

That is particularly the case in northern lands. There, as the year moves towards its end, the increasing cold brings two problems. As the ground freezes, the moisture it contains becomes locked away as ice and can no longer be extracted by the plant's roots. The cells in the leaves are also in danger of freezing. If that happens, the tissues will burst and the leaf will be destroyed. The days are also shortening, reducing the number of hours in every twenty-four when there is enough light for the leaves to work. Food can no longer be manufactured under these conditions. So many plants, in effect, stop functioning.

Oaks and beeches, elms and birch, withdraw the valuable chlorophyll from their leaves. As the green pigment drains away, waste products that have accumulated over the year are revealed and the leaves change colour. In New England, day after day, whole hillsides of maples and aspens flush yellow, orange and red. Sap too is withdrawn. As the leaves dry out, they are sealed off. A hard corky

▷
Maples and oaks flush with autumn colours in the Great Smokey Mountains of Tennessee

deposit develops in the tissues at the base of the leaf stalk. This is brittle and eventually the slightest breeze rustling in the branches is enough to dislodge the leaves and they flutter to the ground.

With their leaves gone, the trees inevitably starve. During the summer when growth was at its most vigorous, trees were adding to their girth. As growth slackened with the approach of autumn, the newly-produced cells became smaller and smaller and by mid-winter their production had ceased altogether. This slow change produces a graduated ring in the wood that is easily seen if the trunk is sectioned. Counting the rings will therefore reveal just how many summers a tree has enjoyed and how many winters it has endured. What is more, the width of the rings – broad in good years and narrow in bad – will provide a record of climatic variation over a tree's lifetime.

Some species of tree, even outside the balmy climates of the tropics, manage to produce a kind of leaf that can survive both

△
The downward slope of their branches and the tough waxy rind of their needle-shaped leaves enable conifers in the Black Forest of Germany to survive the heavy snows of winter

drought and cold. Conifers do so. Many of them grow branches that, instead of rising upwards towards the sky, slope gently downwards. In consequence, snow tends to slide off them and does not accumulate into huge loads that might break them. Their leaves are not flat and broad but needle-shaped. They have a thick waxy rind, very little freezable sap, and pores that are set in the bottom of a deep groove running the length of the needle. Leaves built to this pattern cannot work as productively as a flat leaf during the summer, but they need not be shed during the winter, with all the saving of energy that this economy implies, and they can even manufacture food during the winter if there is a brief spell of warmer sunny weather. But they too work faster during the summer, so they too leave a record of their activity in the trunks of their owners.

▷
The varying width of the annual rings in the trunk of a larch reflect the speed of growth and therefore the climatic conditions of each year of its life

It is from such rings that we know that the oldest tree alive today is one of the bristlecone pines that grow high in the mountains of eastern California. These ancient trees are stunted and ravaged. The tallest of them is only thirty feet high, and many are no more than ten. Much of their gnarled trunks is totally dead. The bark has fallen away, revealing the dried and fissured timber beneath. But some of their branches carry clusters of green needles showing that life still survives in them. The age of any individual can theoretically be measured by driving an auger into its trunk, penetrating to its very heart and extracting the sequence of annual rings. But the

The longest-living organisms on earth: bristlecone pines growing at 10,000 feet in the White Mountains of eastern California
▷▷

trunks of these venerable bristlecone pines are so distorted that it is often difficult to decide where the centre actually lies. Not only that, but conditions high in these mountains where it is extremely cold in winter and arid in summer, are so severe that the pines grow very slowly indeed. In some years, they may not grow at all. Even so, it has been possible, by painstaking work, to establish that a few of these trees are over 4,600 years old. They were already ancient when Columbus landed in the New World. They were in their prime when the first Pharaohs were ruling Egypt; and they germinated at just about the same time that human beings around the eastern end of the Mediterranean were discovering how they could themselves plant seeds and settle down as farmers.

It is a conifer, too, that has a claim to be the most massive organism that the world has ever seen. Elsewhere in the Californian mountains, at somewhat lower altitudes, stand groves of giant sequoias. Some are so big, so nobly impressive that they have their own individual names. One is the General Sherman. It stands 290 feet tall. Its girth, measured at six feet above the ground, is nearly eighty feet. Its trunk, branches, foliage and roots, between them are estimated to weigh over six thousand tons. And this stupendous unparalleled accumulation of organic tissue has all been produced from the simplest and most abundant of ingredients by the strange chemistry, unique to plants, that they conduct within their leaves.

▷
*The giant sequoia
"General Grant"
is about 2,500
years old and
stands 267 feet tall
in King's Canyon,
California. It has a
circumference at
ground level of
108 feet and its
lowest large
branch is 129 feet
above the ground*

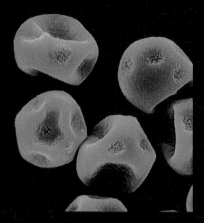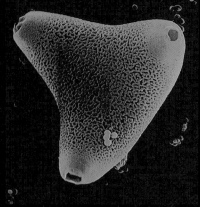
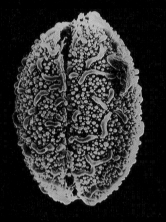
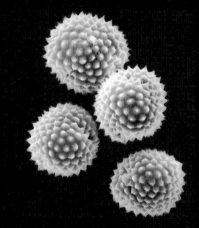
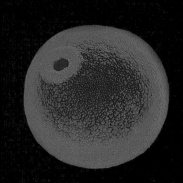

3

FLOWERING

POLLEN grains are truly extraordinary objects. They are microscopic, the size of dust particles. To put their dimensions more precisely, they range in size from 20 to 250 micrometres – and a micrometre is a thousandth of a millimetre. They are produced in astronomical, indeed ungraspable numbers. A single birch catkin can contain five and a half million of them. Since a birch tree may carry several thousand catkins, the statistics of pollen production by several thousand trees in a whole birch wood defies imagination. The grains vary in shape. Some are spherical, others ovoid. Some are ribbed or spiked like grapnels. They may resemble plump cushions or shallow bowls. Miniscule though they are, their surface is often intricately patterned and sculptured – crazed with meandering lines, pocked with tiny circles, diced with intricate geometric figures.

These patterns are so individual and characteristic that they can often be linked with a particular species of plant. The outer rind that carries them is composed of a substance so stable and so resistant to rotting that it may survive for tens of thousands of years and still be recognisable. So by sampling successive layers of peat in a bog and extracting, identifying and counting the pollen grains under the microscope, it is possible to chart the ecological history of an area and detail the arrival, the flourishing and the departure of different plant species.

Because pollen grains are so small and discharged in such quantity from a flower, and because those that are successful ultimately unite with a much larger reproductive cell within another flower, pollen is conventionally described as being a flower's male cells, and the stamens, which produce it, as the male organs. The female

◁

The multitudinous shapes of pollen grains (colours are added):

1	2	3
4	5	6
7	8	9
10	11	12

1   plantain
2   leucospermum
3   buttercup
4   iris
5   ox-eye daisy
6   geranium
7   nettle
8   ragweed
9   sycamore
10   water-lily
11   hollyhock
12   love-grass

organs, which may or may not be present in the same flower, consist of an ovary containing the eggs, and a thin pillar leading up from it, the style, which has a sensitive pad at the top, the stigma. When a pollen grain lands on the stigma there is a subtle interaction between the two, as a result of which the pollen grain extrudes a tiny tube which grows down through the length of the style. When this conduit is complete, the male sex cells pass down it and fertilise the eggs in a chamber beneath. The time this takes varies greatly. In a geranium, the whole act can be completed in a few hours. In an orchid, it may take several months.

A stigma will not react to pollen from another species. Since the physical shape of the pollen grains is so distinctive, it is tempting to think that the recognition between the two is a geometric one analogous to the way that a lock can recognise a key that belongs to it. This may in fact be the case, though if so it is only part of the mechanism of recognition. Other biochemical stimulations and responses also play a crucial part.

The consequence of all these factors is that plants are not only able to ignore pollen that comes from alien species, but in some cases, they can even distinguish between a pollen grain that has been produced by themselves and one from another individual of their own kind. And that means that, when appropriate, they can avoid self-fertilisation.

◇

If a flowering plant is to reproduce sexually, it must ensure that its pollen reaches the style of another individual of the same species. The smallest pollen grains can easily be carried by the wind and a number of plants – grasses and sedges, conifers, and many broad-leaved trees, such as walnut, oak, birch, poplar and hazel – rely on the wind to do that. The pollen of some species of pine has bladders that help it to fly. Those plants that rely on the wind for transport produce small inconspicuous flowers. Indeed some are so modest and undramatic, they may not be recognised as flowers at all. Those of grasses consist of no more than tiny clusters of dry brown or greenish scales from which the stamens protrude when the right

▷
A flowering stem of meadow grass releases its pollen into the wind

moment comes. Their stigmas which have to intercept flying pollen grains are particularly elaborate, often shaped like combs. The biggest of all are those produced by maize. They hang down and are called, very aptly, tassels. Wind-pollinated trees such as hazel usually produce their tiny flowers early in the year, before they put out their leaves, and as a result the wind is able to gather the pollen without hindrance and the grains do not get trapped in the foliage.

Wind is a very effective transporter. It can take the tiny dry grains as high as 19,000 feet and carry them for three thousand miles or so away from their parents. But it is totally haphazard. So the overwhelming proportion of the millions of pollen grains produced by a single plant will fail to reach the stigma of another and therefore be wasted. Since pollen is rich in oils and proteins, and producing it constitutes a significant expense in a plant's economy, this represents a very considerable loss.

◁
Pine trees produce pollen in such quantity that here on the forested shores of a lake in Finland, it forms thick curds

Other plants adopt a different strategy. To reduce the squandering of pollen they invest in devices that recruit animal messengers who collect it and deliver it directly to the female parts of others. A plant will almost certainly be competing with its neighbours of the same species to attract the attention of such messengers. Those that advertise more successfully will leave more offspring, so the competition escalates and over many generations the advertisements become more and more striking. A similar situation occurs among male polygamous birds who compete with one another for the attentions of females with showy displays. Among birds, this rivalry produces the spectacular plumage of peacocks and birds of paradise. Among plants it has led to the development of glorious flowers.

◇

A messenger needs a wage. The simplest way of paying is to allow it to take a percentage of what it is carrying. Pollen, after all, is very nutritious. And that, it seems, was one of the earliest systems that developed even before the appearance of flowers.

Cycads are antique. Dinosaurs fed on them. Male cycads produce their pollen in an enormous cone-shaped structure that develops in the centre of the crown of stiff palm-like leaves. The majority of species still use the ancient and simple distribution technique of allowing the pollen to tumble out and the wind to catch it and carry it away. A few, however, exploit the insects that were already flying in considerable number and variety at the time the first cycads evolved. No plant on earth at that time had yet evolved colourful flowers. Nor had any, as far as we know, developed structures that might produce an irresistibly attractive perfume. But some, maybe, summoned their pollinators by a method which one of their species practises even today. When its pollen is ready for distribution, this cycad raises the temperature of its central cone by a good two degrees. That attracts the attention of weevils. They alight on the cone and feast on the spilling pollen, getting themselves covered with it in the process. Then away they fly to find another meal in the centre of another cycad, taking the pollen with them and so delivering it in a much more economical way than the wind would do.

Water-lilies are descendants of one of the first families to produce true flowers. They still retain the ancient practice of rewarding the couriers with a proportion of their message. They too are fertilised by beetles and most provide little payment other than the pollen itself. But economies can be made in this system.

One is to prevent the pollen from being available to all and sundry, who might take it to inappropriate addresses, and instead to develop an exclusive arrangement with just one species of messenger who can be relied upon to deliver it to the only places where it can be effective, that is to say to other flowers of the same species.

A pink gentian grows in southern Africa, which is pollinated by handsome furry carpenter bees. The flowers of the gentian spread their petals wide, revealing to all a curving white style and three large stamens. Each stamen ends in a long thick anther that seems to be covered in yellow pollen, an obvious temptation to any passing pollen-feeding insect. But that is something of an illusion. The yellow anther is hollow and the pollen is held inside. The only way it can escape is through a tiny hole right at the top of the anther and there is only one way of extracting it. The bee knows how.

It arrives at the flower making a high-pitched buzzing noise with its wings as most bees do. As it alights on an anther, it continues beating its wings but lowers the frequency so that the note of its buzz suddenly falls to approximately middle C. This causes the anther to vibrate at just the right frequency needed to release the pollen and the grains spout out of the hole at the top in a yellow fountain. The bee then industriously gathers it up and packs it into the carrying baskets on its back legs.

Only these bees buzz at this frequency; so only these bees can harvest this pollen. But there is a further refinement in this customised courier service. There is no way a bee can tell whether one of the flowers has lost all its pollen, short of landing on it and shaking its anthers. And that the bees do repeatedly. They quickly discover if none is left, but by that time they have stayed long enough to transfer pollen that they have carelessly collected on their furry bodies to the style of the flower. So in these cases a flower may receive its fertilising pollen without paying any cash on delivery, as is usually required.

There is another way of making savings. Much of the cost of producing pollen is due to its expensive genetic ingredients. Omit those and a powder closely resembling pollen can be produced quite cheaply. And that is precisely the tactic used by tibouchina, a South American shrub. It develops two different kinds of stamens. One kind is large, white, and prominent and it is these that produce this sterile imitation pollen. A bee, when it arrives, ignores smaller pink stamens that sprout close to the flower's landing platform. In

△

*Melastoma, like its
close relative
tibouchina, has two
kinds of stamens,
only one of which is
sexually potent -
the smaller inner
group*

its hurry to start feeding on the white stamens, it walks right over the pink ones. But as it does so, they dust its underside with an economical amount of the expensive sexually-effective pollen.

The most widely practised economy of all, however, is to provide payment that is nothing more than sweetened water – nectar. A plant produces this from special glands, nectaries, that are usually hidden deep in the depths of a flower. Positioning them in this way has two advantages. It reduces loss of nectar by evaporation or dilution by rain; and it compels a visiting messenger to brush past the anthers and so collect its load of pollen. But this reward has to be advertised; and that is the function of the petals.

◇

Insects were probably the first couriers to be used by plants and they remain to this day the most numerous kind. Flowers that employ them must necessarily tailor their advertisements to match insect senses. Most insects have a very highly developed sense of smell, so they can be attracted by perfume. Many also have excellent vision. Their eyes, however, are very different from ours, being

△

*An evening
primrose in normal
light (left) appears
almost unmarked,
but ultra-violet
light reveals clear
pointers to its
reward of nectar*

◁

*Landing
instructions for
pollinating insects
are provided by the
mountain laurel
from North
America (above)
and the Spanish iris
(below) from the
Pyrenees*

made up of a mosaic of several hundred tiny elements. Each of these receives a narrow beam of light and registers no more of it than its intensity, but all together they produce a complete if a somewhat granular picture. And there is a further difference – in the perception of colour. At the red end of the spectrum, the insect eye is not as sensitive as ours. Most insects are unable to distinguish between red and black as we can. At the other end, the blue end, they are very much more sensitive than we are and can detect ultra-violet colours that are totally invisible to us. So if we wish to get some idea of an insect's perception of a particular bloom, we should not neglect to look at it in a way that makes ultra-violet visible to us. That can be done using special film and filters and when we do that, hitherto unsuspected markings may appear on the petals.

Many insect-pollinated flowers, particularly those that have concealed their nectaries, perhaps at the end of a long tube, have dots and lines which lead from the outer lip, where an insect might alight, to the nectar within. Foxgloves and irises, pansies and rhododendrons are obvious examples. These marks are plainly guidelines akin to those we ourselves put on airport runways. Photograph a gentian with film sensitive to ultraviolet light and what seems to our naked eye to be a plain blue trumpet is revealed to have explicit markings. The meadow cranesbill, a relatively open

The flowerhead of angelica attracts many different insects including, as here, hoverflies, flesh flies and green bluebottles

flower that might not seem to require any special sign-posting, has ultra-violet lines down its purple petals leading to its centre.

Some plants are not very selective in their recruiting and allow many different kinds of insects to collect pollen from them. The broad white flower heads of cow parsley and angelica are often visited simultaneously by butterflies, beetles, and hoverflies, all taking a share of the pollen. Poppies, wood anemones, bramble, buttercup and many other plants that produce relatively simple, widely opening flowers are similarly generous and indiscriminate. But pollen delivered to flowers of another kind is pollen wasted. So many other plants, like the South African gentian and its carpenter bee, have found it advantageous to arrange that their couriers only deliver their pollen to other individual plants of the same species. That can be achieved by developing a flower which holds its nectar so securely that only one kind of insect has access to it. An insect with a monopoly of a rich supply is likely, while that reward is available, to look nowhere else. So partnerships have developed of an increasingly specialised kind in which both members have become so dependent upon one another that were one to disappear, the other would very likely either starve or remain sterile.

In South Africa, the twinspur, a relative of the foxglove unique in its family for having not just one tubular spur but two, rewards its

A bumblebee gathers pollen from a dandelion and collects so much on its fur that some will brush off on to the next flower it visits

pollinators with oil secreted at the far end of each spur. Several closely related species of solitary bees have developed brushes on the tips of their fore-legs with which to mop up this oil. There are several species of twinspurs with different lengths of flowers; and there are corresponding bee species, each with forelegs that exactly match the length of the flowers of one of the twinspur species.

▷
The only insect capable of reaching angraecum's nectar is a hawkmoth. Its tongue, normally kept coiled beneath its head (above) is so long it can be plunged deep (below) into the orchid's spurs

◁
Angraecum, a Madagascan orchid, produces its nectar from the bottom of exceedingly long trailing spurs

The most extreme and celebrated example of this matching between the anatomies of flower and pollinator is that of an orchid and a moth in Madagascar. The scientific name of the orchid is Angraecum sesquipedale. The second word means 'a foot and a half' and refers to the long trailing spurs which hold its nectar. In sober truth, few are quite as long as that, but some approach it. Only

one insect has a proboscis of such a length, a rare species of hawk moth, and that is the orchid's only pollinator.

Orchids have produced the most elaborate pollination systems of all. Indeed, some have created obstacle courses for their couriers of such complexity that it is difficult to imagine why they should go to so much trouble to achieve a result that most other plants reach by comparatively simple means.

The bucket orchid grows high in the canopy of the forests of central America, sitting on the boughs of the great trees. Its flowers are yellow, sometimes plain and sometimes mottled with orange or brown according to the species, and they hang down, half a dozen or so on a stem. The front of the flower is formed by two small wings. These serve as signposts. Behind them hangs the little bucket that gives the plant its name. When a flower opens, two small glands on the stem connecting the bucket to the frontal wings secrete a liquid that drips down and fills the bucket to a depth of about a quarter of an inch. The flowers now give off a sweet heady perfume. Each of the twenty or so species of bucket orchid has its own brand of scent. Although human nostrils cannot distinguish between them, little iridescent bees that live in these forests certainly can. Each species of orchid attracts its own species of bee.

It is only the male bees who respond to the orchid. Its smell seems to excite them greatly and when a flower opens there will soon be several male bees buzzing around it in an agitated way. Before long one will land on the side or the rim of the bucket and make his way to a rounded pad that rises from the rim at the base of the short stem connecting the bucket to the front of the flower. From this pad he scrapes an oily substance which he packs into pockets on his back legs. This is not a food. It is an ointment that he will use to attract females during his elaborate courtship rituals – which is why each species of bee needs its own special brand.

Once he has collected a full load, he tries to fly off. But there can be such a congestion of excited bees in and around the flower, and the surface of the pad is so slippery, that sooner or later, one of the bees loses his footing and tumbles into the fluid at the bottom of the bucket. There is only one way out – a tunnel leading up through the front wall of the bucket to the outside world. On the wall just below this escape hatch there is a little bump. It is the only reasonable

△
*A bee tumbles into
the bucket orchid's
pond*

foothold to be found on the otherwise smooth slippery walls of the bucket and eventually the bee discovers it. Using it as a step, he climbs up and enters the tunnel. It is a very tight fit but he manages to squeeze his way up it. Just as he is about to emerge from the other end and regain his freedom, his back catches on a projection in the roof of the tunnel. This is caused by two lumps of the orchid's coagulated pollen called the pollinia. The bee continues to struggle forward and finally scrapes off the pollinia from the roof of the tunnel so that when he does at last emerge, they are attached securely to his back like a little knapsack. His whole visit may have taken about ten minutes.

Meanwhile, other bees are still feeding on the pad. One may have gone through this obstacle course before in another flower and already have pollinia on his back. If such a one slips into the bucket, then the orchid is lucky, for when he struggles up through the tunnel, a hook on the roof neatly engages on the pollinia and removes them. The orchid, after all the travails of the bees, has been fertilised.

*A bumble bee
makes a smash and
grab raid, stealing
nectar from a
comfrey plant
which it could not
otherwise reach, by
piercing the side of
the flower with its
proboscis*

◁
*A bee, having
survived his swim
in the bucket
orchid's pool,
emerges through its
escape-hatch into
the outside world*

*A New Zealand
gecko drinks nectar
from native flax
and gathers pollen
on its throat*
▷▷

But not all insects dutifully accept the persuasions and directives dictated by flowers. Some have become burglars. Comfrey keeps its nectar in the depths of its tubular flowers. Some bumblebees have prosbosces an inch or so long and they have no difficulty in reaching it. One species, however, that normally drinks from other kinds of flower, has only a short tongue. In some way it has discovered the existence of this hidden treasure. Faced with a comfrey flower, it lands on the exterior of the flower close to its base, chews a hole in it and steals the nectar.

Reptiles, the first backboned animals to wander freely around dry land, appeared many millions of years after the first insects. What proportion of them collected pollen from plants we cannot know but some, surely, must have done so. And some still do. In New Zealand, which land mammals did not reach until they were taken there by human beings, geckos regularly visit the flowers of native flax during the night. They prise open the long petals of the tube-shaped flowers, insert their tongues into the side and sip the nectar. As they do so, they collect yellow pollen on their throats and chins from other flowers growing on the same stem. In some places as many as half a dozen geckos can be found feeding on spikes of newly-opened flax flowers. And there is good evidence that the little reptiles will travel very considerable distances during the night to visit other flowers, taking the pollen with them.

△
*A South African
collared sunbird
avoids collecting
the sticky pollen of
strelitzia when it
drinks nectar*

It is difficult to imagine that the flax or any other plant could rely totally on the geckos as pollinators, for these days they are not very abundant, but in the past, before mammalian predators were introduced into New Zealand, the geckos may well have been sufficiently numerous to have done so very adequately.

In South Africa there is another plant that may have originally used reptiles as pollinators. The bird-of-paradise flower, strelitzia, is notorious for setting very little seed in the wild. In cultivation, solicitous gardeners artfully pollinate it with a paint brush. When that is done, the plant will produce seed in great quantity. It is often said that the flower's natural pollinators are birds and that its bizarre structure is a complex mechanism ensuring that when a bird lands on the blue spike in the centre of the flower, it forces out the anthers which dust pollen all over its chest. But strangely, there are no first-hand accounts of this happening. The birds that habitually collect nectar from the flowers are sunbirds. They seldom if ever land in this way but usually either cling to the side of the flower or hang from the spray of vertical orange petals and then lean down to drink. As a result they do not get touched by pollen. It seems that they deliberately avoid releasing the anthers. And there is a very good reason why they should do so. Strelitzia pollen is moist and stringy and could seriously soil a bird's feathers. And sunbirds are particularly fastidious in their toilet. On the other hand, an animal that lacked the power of flight and had to crawl over the flower to find the nectar, would depress the blue shroud in just the right way to get sticky pollen all over its underside. So maybe strelitzia originally evolved to entice lizards. Since then, however, the lizards have been displaced by more agile nectar feeders, sunbirds, and as a result the flowers are now seldom fertilised naturally.

Birds appeared even later than the reptiles. Indeed, all the evidence suggests that they evolved from them. Today, birds rival insects as pollinators. To enlist their services, however, plants have to use very different methods. Birds lack almost totally a sense of smell. Perfume would be wasted on them and flowers seeking to attract them do not waste energy in producing it. On the other hand, bird eyes are very acute and much more like ours than those of insects. Plants, when they first advertised to insects, tended to neglect the red end of the spectrum since insects are largely insensitive to it. Red was therefore available for advertising to birds and many plants used it in this way. Birds are, of course, much bigger than

Australian rainbow lorikeets, attracted by the scarlet flowers of a grevillea, feast on nectar
▽

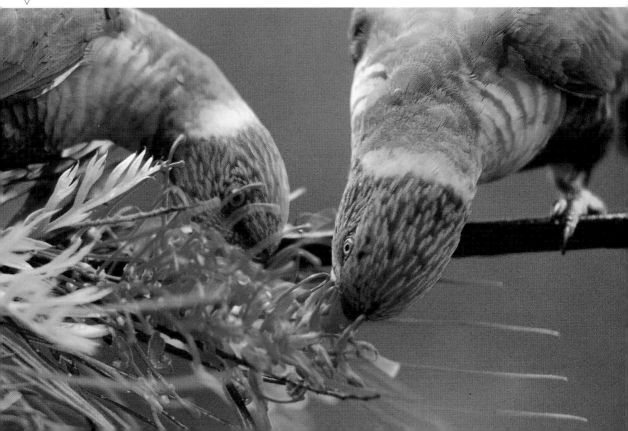

insects and the plants that employ them must also make special provision for that fact. Their flowers must be large enough to accommodate the head of a bird as it seeks nectar and coincidentally collects its load of pollen, and the petals must be relatively strong to withstand such vigorous treatment. So if a flower is large, robust, red and lacks smell, it is very likely that it is pollinated by birds.

Most birds need something on which to stand as they take their drinks. Trees, such as the flame of the forest and the African tulip tree, carry their magnificent scarlet flowers on branches that are quite strong enough to support a bird, but smaller plants may have to make special arrangements. Kangaroo-paws are a western Australian group of ground-living plants, related to lilies, with handsome tubular flowers. All are pollinated by birds. Some are only a few inches high and they point their flowers downwards so that a bird, hopping along the ground, has no difficulty in reaching up with its beak to sip nectar from them. But some species grow so tall that their flowers are far beyond the reach of a bird on the ground. The stem from which their flowers sprout, however, is far stouter and stronger than seems necessary to support blossom. This is because it has an additional function. It has to carry the weight of a pollinating bird and it is, in fact, so rigid that honey-eaters have no hesitation in perching on it in order to collect their drinks.

Once plants have attracted a bird, they have to ensure that it does not collect its wage and then leave without its load of pollen. If the flower is tubular in shape – and many bird-pollinated flowers are – then it is not very difficult to position the stamens so that when a bird thrusts its head inside to reach for the nectar, its forehead or its breast are dusted with pollen. But some flowers take no chances and have mechanisms to ensure that their visitors are stabbed, clouted, sprayed or showered with pollen.

One of the tropical species of mistletoe keeps its bright red flowers tightly closed until it is visited by a thirsty and inquisitive bird. Its visitor knows how to open them and inserts its beak into a slit in the bud. Immediately, the bud springs open and a battery of anthers flip down and strike the bird's forehead. Another species in the same family stores its pollen in the roof of its flower. As a bird lands, its weight triggers the chamber so that it opens explosively and showers pollen all over the bird's forehead.

◁
A tawny-crowned honey-eater utilises the robust stem of Mangels' kangaroo-paw to reach the flower. West Australia

△
A rufous hummingbird, as it collects nectar from an aquilegia is given a liberal dusting of pollen on its chin

Some birds recruited by flowers have specialised in nectar feeding and eat nothing else, except for tiny insects. In Africa, they include sunbirds, sugar birds and honey-eaters. They are all so small that they can perch on the flower itself. They have thin beaks which can be inserted into the tiny nectaries accurately and easily. Their tongues are long and can collect the nectar with quick flicks. Their digestion has now become so adapted to their particular diet that they cannot cope with other foods.

The most highly specialised of all nectar-feeding birds, however, are South American – hummingbirds. They closely resemble the African sunbirds in the general shape of their body, but they have one additional talent. They can beat their wings so swiftly and articulate them so accurately that they can hang in the air in front of a flower. South American plants, in response, attract them with delicate flowers, suspended from the end of long thin stems and facing outwards so that they can only be entered from the air.

The rate at which such a flower supplies its nectar has to be carefully controlled. If the plant is miserly and produces very little, a bird will not find it worthwhile calling. If it is too generous, then the bird might be so satisfied after its visit that it will not hurry to seek more nectar elsewhere and so fail to deliver the pollen swiftly. Many plants have arrived at such a perfect compromise between these two extremes that the hummingbirds pollinating them are compelled to keep continuously active, rushing from one flower to another, getting just enough each time to fuel their high-energy flying equipment with just sufficient calories left over to make the trip profitable. At night, when they cannot see to fly and the flowers have closed, the birds have no alternative but to shut down all their systems, lower their body temperature and, in effect, hibernate until dawn.

Nectar is sometimes stolen even in the world of the humming-birds. Another drab little bird that lives alongside them in the Andes has developed special tools to assist it in burglary. It is called, accurately enough, a flower-piercer. The upper half of its beak is notched along its edge and hooked at the end. The lower half is rather shorter and very sharply pointed. The bird lands on or beside a tubular flower and snags it with its hook. Holding the flower steady in this way, it then stabs it with the lower part of its beak and flicks its tongue inside to steal the honey.

Nearly all of these nectar-feeding birds live in the tropics. That is no accident. In colder parts of the world, flowering is restricted to summer. Any specialist nectar-feeder would die of starvation in winter. Insects that feed on nectar can survive the winter either as eggs or dormant larvae, or by hibernating. But birds have never developed those abilities. Nectar-feeding birds must therefore have a sequence of different flowers to sustain them throughout the year. To find them, many have to travel, following the seasons. So in Australia, where a high proportion of birds feed on nectar, many migrate slowly across the continent keeping pace with the changing seasons in order to feed continuously on nectar. In the Americas in July and August, hummingbirds fly northward and, at the very height of summer, even briefly visit the northern United States.

These days, their stay is longer than it used to be, for now they can find sugary liquid not only in the heart of flowers, but in bottles hung outside the homes of bird-loving human beings.

Mammals appeared even more recently than birds in evolutionary history. Many are so big and clumsy when compared to birds or insects, that they seem ill-suited to be pollinators. Yet even so a few of them have been pressed into service by plants. Proteas, in southern Africa, are for the most part pollinated by sunbirds and therefore, as you might expect, they have large robust flowers often conspicuously marked with red that they hoist high in the air. But one or two species in the family develop flowers that are very different. They are dully coloured, occur underneath the bush largely shrouded by the foliage above, and point downwards. Their nectar is collected at night by small rock mice and shrews. For the animals, this just is a seasonal treat lasting for only a few weeks, after which they have to go back to other foods. For the proteas, however, it is an invaluable service at a crucial time.

The traveller's palm is one of Madagascar's most spectacular and decorative plants. It sprouts a single vertical fan of huge leaves that can be thirty feet high. Its flowers, which appear in clusters from the axils of these leaves, have large chambers into which nectar is secreted in great quantity during the twenty-four hours that the flower's stigma is receptive. And it is visited by an animal that matches the tree for spectacular beauty, a ruffed lemur. Lemurs are primitive relations of monkeys. This one is the size of a spaniel, though more lightly built and has long soft fur in dramatic patches of either red and white or black and white. When it arrives, usually descending from the canopy of the surrounding forest, it quickly locates a flower that has just opened, and seizes the bracts, the protective leaf-like structures that grow outside a flower's ring of petals, pulling them apart with its hands to get to the flower within. That it opens with its teeth. Then it pushes its muzzle inside and drinks the nectar. The plant produces its flowers in considerable numbers day after day for two or three months and while it is doing so, nectar is the lemur's major food. It has a much longer snout and much longer tongue than most other lemurs. No insect, reptile or bird in Madagascar seems to have the strength to pull apart the

◁

A pygmy possum collects nectar from eucalyptus blossom. South-east Australia

bracts around the flowers, so it seems very likely indeed that lemur and tree have evolved together in partnership.

Such relationships with mammals are frequent in Australia. There, at least twenty-one species of marsupials take nectar. The pygmy possum regularly collects it to sweeten its meals of insects. The honey possum feeds on little else and has become so adapted to the diet that its teeth have become rudimentary and its jaw bones little more than splinters. Its tongue, however, has developed a brush-like surface with which it gathers nectar from a great number of plants - grevilleas, banksias, eucalypts, and some species of kangaroo-paws - which between them keep it fed the year round.

One group of mammals has been particularly useful to plants – the mammalian equivalent of birds, bats. Small bats, equipped with sonar, are essentially insect-eaters. It is the larger kind, with big eyes, that serve the plants as pollinators. To attract them, flowers must open at night and be pale in colour so that they are easily visible in the darkness. Their perfume must be a smell that appeals to mammalian nostrils – yeasty, musty, rancid, even reminiscent of urine. Baobabs produce flowers that are all of these things. A tropical liana, freycinetia, provides the bats with not only nectar and pollen but a special reward of big juicy bracts. Some of the fruit bats, in their turn, have evolved characteristics that make them particularly efficient at collecting nectar. Macroglossus means simply big-tongued and the bats that carry that name have a tongue as long as their body with a brush-like surface that enables them to scoop up nectar and pollen in great quantities.

Nearly all wild bananas are pollinated by bats. Their tubular flowers are produced in a line on a long dangling stalk. Each rank is protected by a long sheath-like bract. Every night, the topmost bract rises to a horizontal position, exposing a line of flowers beneath. Initially, these flowers are female and bats, coming to sup their nectar, transfer on to them pollen which they carry on their fur. The next morning, the petals and the bract fall off, leaving the fertilised eggs in their ovaries to develop into fruit. After a few nights, all the female flowers on a particular stem have been exposed. Those that grow farther down the stem are all male. But the same nightly sequence of events continues. Another bract rises to expose a new set of flowers and another procession of bats comes

▷

A long-nosed bat, although equipped with an exceptionally long tongue, has to thrust its head deep into a cactus flower in order to reach the nectar and as a result gets pollen all over its face

to collect their nectar. This time they don't deliver pollen but collect it.

Cacti, too, favour bats as pollinators. This is only to be expected. In the dry hot deserts where cacti grow, very few animals of any kind are active during the oven-hot day. Many more potential messengers are abroad at night. So the organ-pipe and cardon cacti open their flowers at dusk and shut them again during the morning. By this time they may well have been visited by bats, particularly since they arrange their flowering season to coincide with the northward migration of bats from Mexico up to the southern United States. For the bats, the cacti with their abundant nectar provide an invaluable pit-stop on their long, eight hundred mile journey. For the cacti, the bats are a transient but invaluable regiment of messengers.

◇

So plants reward all kinds of animals – bats and birds and overwhelmingly, insects – for carrying their pollen. The arrangement seems fair. But there is no morality in the natural world and there are plants that achieve the same result without rewarding their couriers in any way. Indeed, some trap and seemingly punish them.

Orchids, in particular, have developed a range of enticements that in the event provide no reward whatsoever for those that succumb. The oncidiums of South America, often called popularly the dancing lady orchids, produce a cloud of tiny flowers on long branched spikes and are so delicately balanced on their stalks that they dance about in the slightest breeze. Small bees live in the same forests, the males of which are exceedingly pugnacious in defending their territories. When the oncidium produces its spray of flowers, the bees charge in to them, attacking them as if they were rivals. And in the process, they both gather pollen and dispense it.

Rothschild's slipper orchid that grows on Mount Kinabalu in Borneo has two long twisted wings stretching horizontally on either side of the slipper-shaped cup that gives the members of its family their name. This carries markings on the front that apparently resemble a little flock of aphids for a fly, which habitually lays eggs among aphids so that its grubs may parasitise them, also lays its

△
*Rothschild's slipper
orchid is pollinated
by flies seeking an
advantageous place
for their eggs*

eggs on this particular place on the orchid. Having done so, it becomes trapped in the cup and is only able to escape by completing an obstacle course, not unlike that inflicted by the bucket orchid on its bees.

European orchids cannot compete in spectacular flamboyant beauty with their tropical relations. Not for them huge flaring skirts and glamorous turbans, quivering diadems or elegant pennants. The mirror orchid of the western Mediterranean is typical of many. It is a ground-dwelling plant about a foot high which produces a few flowers on a single stem. These have an oval lip that glistens with an unusual metallic violet-blue colour and has a yellow border fringed with long red hairs. There are two smaller side lobes rather like insect wings. Each flower looks, in fact, remarkably like one of

the species of large wasp or bee that are common in the areas where it grows. The function of this mimicry is sensational. The flower is making sexual suggestions to the male bees. It does so even more effectively than we ourselves might realise for it also releases a chemical signal, a pheromone, which closely resembles that emitted by sexually receptive female bees. That can be demonstrated by covering one of these orchids with a cloth. Even though it is invisible male bees are attracted to it and crawl agitatedly all over it, seeking the source of this exciting and provocative smell.

If and when a male bee finds the flower, he settles upon the lip, grasping it in exactly the same way as he grasps a female bee, and tries to copulate, thrusting the tip of his abdomen into the fringe of long hairs at the end of the lip. He fails, of course, but in the process, a curved column that houses both male and female organs, descends from the top of the orchid and glues a pair of pollinia to his head. If the next orchid he visits has already despatched its pollinia, then the column will pick up the one he carries and the orchid is fertilised.

There are nearly a hundred identifiably different kinds of orchids of this type in Europe, each with its own impersonating pattern and its own species of insect dupe. The hairs on the lip of the mirror orchid, like many others, point downwards and suggest to the male bee that his bogus mate is hanging on the flower with her head pointing upwards. But another group of these orchids, including

△
The Cyprus bee orchid (left) mimics the appearance of the species of bee (right) that pollinates it with such accuracy that no other bees are attracted to it

▷
The mirror orchid imitates the female of its bee partner with a blue patch that resembles the sheen of the bee's wings

▷
A male bee, stimulated by this image as well as by the orchid's perfume, lands in the correct position for copulation

▷
— and causes the column of the orchid to snap forward and clip the pollinia on the bee's head

the yellow bee orchid, have lip hairs that point in the opposite direction. The male insects that land on them clearly have the impression that their females have settled head-down, for they themselves swivel round to be suitably placed for copulation. In this position a male gets saddled with the pollinia not on his head but on his abdomen.

The fact that there are both front-loaders and back-loaders among these orchids allows them to share pollinators. One orchid mimics a head-up female bee: another species mimics the same kind of bee but head-down. So an individual bee of this species can get

△
The male bee attempting copulation with a yellow bee orchid receives the pollinia on his abdomen

This bee, having previously visited a head-up mimic is saddled with a double load
▽

encumbered with two different kinds of pollinia, one on his head and one on his abdomen.

These couplings are demonstrably unsatisfactory for the male wasp or bee. He quickly learns that the perfume which lured him to his unresponsive partner is not to be trusted. And that, of course, might reduce his value as a pollinator, for having been saddled with pollinia, he may not visit other orchid plants and deliver them. However, all individual plants of one species, while they produce a scent that mimics the female pheromone in its essentials, do not smell exactly the same. Each plant differs sufficiently from others to suggest to the bee that this next one, with a slightly different fragrance, will give him the satisfaction that has eluded him so far. But after visiting four or five different plants, he has learned his lesson – the whole lot that smell in this general way are useless and he visits them no more. But by that time, he is likely to have done what the orchids required of him.

The most extraordinary of these sexual deceptions is played upon an Australian wasp. It belongs to a family, the thynnids, the females of which feed on the grubs of scarab beetles. The grubs live in the soil, eating the roots of plants, so a female wasp has to dig to find them and she spends all her early life underground seeking them. Wings are an encumbrance to a digger and she has none. When she is fully grown and the time comes to mate, she tunnels her way to the surface, clambers up the stem of a nearby plant and releases her pheromone. As soon as a male detects this, he flies up-wind towards her, keeping the pheromone strong in his antennae, until he finds her. Then he lands on her back. But instead of mating immediately, he picks her up bodily and flies off with her. And there, in mid-air,

▷
A male thynnid wasp carries his wingless female on to a flower for a nuptial drink of nectar

they copulate. He then gallantly takes her on a tour of all the best feeding spots in the area, visiting flower after flower and giving her the first and only drink of nectar in her life. This may take him several hours, but the service is very important for it provides her with the sustenance that she needs to produce the eggs in which he now has a share and which she will lay in a few day's time when she returns underground.

The dragon orchid has managed to insert itself into this complicated succession of events. The lip of its flower mimics very competently the appearance of the wingless female wasp sitting plumply and expectantly on her stem. It is the right sort of colour with the right markings. It even gives off a perfume that closely resembles her pheromone. Above it, however, hangs an additional feature, the curving column containing both the orchids's anthers and its style. Whether the resemblance of the whole construction to a female wasp would be effective set against a real female is questionable, but the orchid does not risk such a comparison. The male wasps are flying and hunting for insects some weeks before their females are ready to emerge from the ground and it is during this period that the orchid opens its flowers.

A male wasp, fully adult and ready to mate, is immediately attracted by the imitation pheromone. Without hesitation, he lands on the bogus female and tries to take off with her. But what he grips so firmly with his legs is, of course, hinged to the column of the

A male thynnid wasp attempts to mate with the dragon orchid's impersonation of his female and is tipped up to receive his pollen
▽

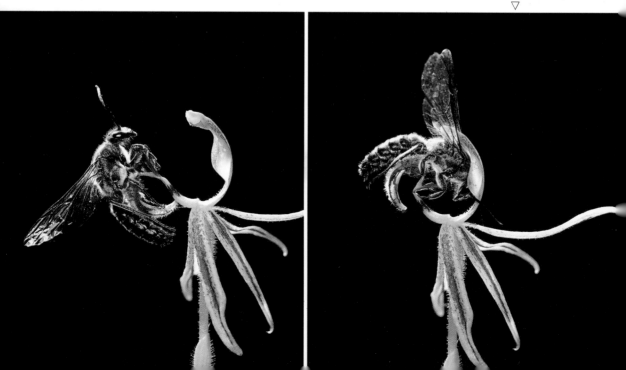

flower and his vigorous attempt to carry off his bride results only in him being tipped head-down so that his back smacks the style on the tip of the column. As it does so the orchid's pollinia are fixed to his back. This rough handling does not seem to deter him, for having discovered that what he thought was a female was no such thing, he flies off and is quite likely to be deceived a second time. If he is, then his next somersault in an orchid will remove the pollinia. He may not have scored sexually, but the orchid has.

◇

Orchids have made something of a speciality of sexually bamboozling their pollinators. Arums have become expert in taking them prisoners. They belong to a big family distributed throughout the tropics with just a few species growing in more temperate parts. The most familiar of them is a South African species known as the arum lily – misleadingly so, for arums are not at all closely related to lilies. It has a virginally white trumpet called a spathe, from the centre of which emerges a long yellow rod, the spadix. Technically speaking, this bloom should be called an inflorescence, for it is not a single flower but a whole group of them. They sprout around the base of the spadix and are enclosed by the spathe. In some countries, people display bunches of arum lilies at funerals. That association with death is, perhaps, unwittingly apt for although the arum lily itself is not implicated in such crimes, many of its relations are kidnappers and even murderers.

The dead horse arum grows on the islands of Corsica and Sardinia in the Mediterranean, often near a colony of gulls. At the height of the birds' breeding season, it produces its flower. The spathe, far from being an immaculate white, is greyish purple, blotched and streaked with pink, covered with coarse dark red hairs and the size of a dinner plate. It gives off a smell remarkably like the stench that comes from carrion. It resembles, in short, a piece of rotting flesh.

A gull colony is normally buzzing with blow-flies. They have lots of food for themselves and their grubs – dead chicks, broken and rotting eggs, droppings, and decaying fish that have been brought back for the chicks by their parents but have somehow missed their mark. The blow-flies swarm over this new dish. As they wander over the surface of the spathe, they come to the lower part of the spadix which disappears into a hole from which the smell is coming. Blow-flies are familiar with such features. It could be an empty eye-socket or a hole pecked in the belly of a dead sheep by a carrion-feeding bird. Such apertures are entrances to a corpse's interior, the best and safest place for the flies to feast and lay their eggs. In they go. They crawl down the spadix, forcing their way past a cluster of thin spikes and hairs and clamber down into the chamber beneath. In the darkness, they cross first a ring of small male flowers that encircle the spadix, then further down a band of horizontal spikes, and below that another encircling band of small female flowers. And then they reach the bottom.

It is warm and foetid, as it must be within a rotting corpse. The exit up the spadix is partially blocked by the hairs but the flies are apparently in no mood to escape. All the conditions seem exactly right for egg-laying. Many of the females do so and a pile of eggs accumulates on the floor. These may eventually hatch but the grubs will die, for there is nothing here for them to eat. The plant would gain nothing by providing them with food. But it does need the services of the adults, and to make sure that they do not die yet, the female flowers exude nectar for them. Those flies that have visited such an arum before will have brought pollen with them so, as they drink from the female flowers, they fertilise them. By now the chamber may be so full of flies that some of them suffocate and die. But the exit has become so clogged that no escape is possible.

About a day after the flower opened, the female flowers cease being receptive and cut off their nectar supply. Only now, do the male flowers in the highest band on the spadix become mature and release their pollen. All the female flowers are likely to have been pollinated already by the flies and in any case, since they are no longer receptive, there is no danger of them being fertilised by their own pollen. The surviving flies, clambering around in the darkness, inevitably become covered with pollen. At last, they can be released. The hairs around the entrance wither and the flies escape, taking with them fresh loads of pollen to deposit elsewhere.

▷
A deserted gull's nest, with dead chicks and broken eggs, attracts swarms of flies. Close by, the dead horse arum, reeking of rotten flesh, offers its imitation of a corpse

◇

The biggest of all the arum family is truly a monster. If an inflorescence may be regarded as a single flower, as it is, surely, by those without botanical inhibitions, then that produced by the titan arum must surely be the largest flower in the world. It grows only in the rain forests of central Sumatra in Indonesia. Like all other arums, it has a trumpet-shaped spathe from the centre of which projects a spadix. But the titan's spathe is three feet across with its lip four feet above the ground and its spadix is nine feet tall. You might suppose that a plant with such spectacular world-beating dimensions would be so huge and so celebrated that it would be easy to find. Not so.

The first European to record seeing it was an Italian botanist, Odoardo Beccari who, in 1878, was exploring and collecting plants in Sumatra. He tried to dig up his extraordinary discovery and found that the giant flower had sprung from a corm, a food storage organ formed from its hugely swollen underground stem. This was roughly spherical with a circumference of nearly five feet and was so heavy that the two men who had dug it out had to struggle to lift it. One of them slipped and the gigantic corm broke. This is not surprising for the titan's corm consists almost entirely of vegetable fat and has minimal internal structure. Once its delicate skin is broken, as it can easily be if it is handled roughly, it will rot into a mound of mush in a matter of days.

Beccari did, however, succeed in finding others that presumably were smaller and more manageable for he was able to send them to botanic gardens in Europe. One reached Kew and a year later flowered. But this early success has seldom been repeated. The plant, it seems, usually dies after flowering. No cultivated specimen has ever produced fertile seed so it has not been possible to establish this wonder in European botanic gardens.

Nor is it easy to locate one in the forests that are its natural home. The seedlings produce a leaf that is more like a small tree than a leaf. It rises vertically on a strong round glossy pillar, green speckled with white and more like a trunk than a stem. This divides at the top into three branches which bear smaller leaflets, forming a wide umbrella. A full-grown leaf may stand twenty feet tall and form a canopy fifteen feet across. Every year the plant manufactures food in the huge leaf and adds to the food store in its swelling corm.

▷
The titan arum, the day after it has opened to the full, closes its spathe around its huge spadix

And every year the leaf withers and is regrown. After several years – said by some to be about seven – its leaf decays for the last time and the plant rests for some six months. Nothing remains on the forest floor to indicate where the corm might lie. Then at no particular time of the year or any predictable moment, a giant bud emerges from the bare ground. It may pause, unopen, for a number of days and then suddenly, at great speed, growing several inches a day, the bloom develops to its full height. The spadix pushes up through the folds of the spathe and the spathe itself unfurls.

Two days later, the structure collapses. The tall grey spadix, which is filled with cobweb-like support fibres, becomes flaccid, topples forward and droops over the margin of the spathe. The spathe itself contracts inwards and its upper margins start to twist around the lower part of the spadix, clasping it so tightly that a huge water-tight bag is created. Safe inside it, the ovaries of the fertilised female flowers begin to swell. The basal stem supporting the whole structure, however, continues to grow, increasing in girth and lifting the great pear-shaped bag higher and higher into the air.

After some time, the bag decays and falls away, unveiling several thousand huge berries, each up to six inches long that form a band around the tall pillar. They then turn a brilliant scarlet. Hornbills now come to feast on this sumptuous offering of fruit and take the seeds for miles through the forest before voiding them with their droppings.

Finding a flower with such a brief life is clearly not easy. Local people do not necessarily remember the exact spot in the dense forest where its tall leaf once stood. Even if they do, they cannot be certain that the plant had reached maturity and that its next bud, when it might appear, would produce not a leaf but a flower. So finding a titan arum in flower is a never-to-be-forgotten thrill. The one we photographed stood on a steep slope in thick forest, just above a river. Its spathe was shaped like an inverted bell with its point close to the ground. It was strengthened by long white ribs, like the spokes of a half-opened upside-down umbrella. Its upper margin was frilled. Outside, it was a creamy green, but inside an intense and glowing crimson. From the centre of this rose the huge spadix, like a wrinkled greyish spire. It was so out of scale with every other plant around it that it seemed to belong to another

▷

The female flowers of the titan arum clustered around the base of its spadix. A small sweat bee flies around them with pollen packed in its leg pouches. Above are the yellow male flowers

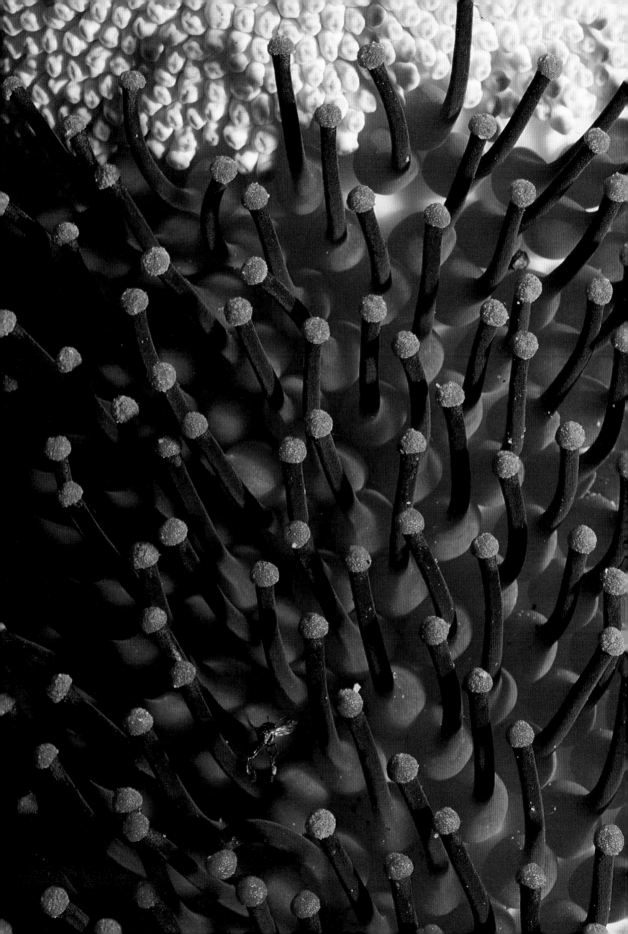

world, to have landed perhaps from outer space. For some indefinable reason I felt that it would not have been surprising to see it make some convulsive movement. Indeed, the pleats of the spathe must have been expanding outwards imperceptibly, for it was certainly marginally wider after about an hour.

Looking down into its depths, there seemed to be a light shining up from the bottom. The illusion was created by a fine shading of the red pigment that turned to white at the lowest point. If any insect flying in the neighbourhood was positively attracted by bright light – and there are many which are – then the spathe's colouring might have been an optical inducement to fly down to the depths of the great funnel and reach the flowers clustered around the base of the spadix.

The titan's inflorescence is said to give off a revolting stench, but the bloom we found smelt only mildly of rotting fish. Perhaps this was because it was already a day old and it had produced its most pungent aroma as soon as it opened, so as to attract its pollinators with the minimum delay. As we sat beside it, the smell seemed to come in waves. Sometimes it was strong; sometimes it faded. There was no wind in the forest, so we had to conclude that the flower was sending out its perfume in pulses.

But to whom? No pollinators appeared, though we waited until the approach of darkness compelled us to start on the long walk out of the forest. We returned the following day. The spathe had closed up around the spadix but on one side the pleats drooped outwards so that we could see the flowers in its heart. The topmost band of cream-coloured male flowers encircled the round base of the spadix like a piece of tightly woven beadwork. Below them stretched another deeper band of rather larger and more richly coloured beads, the female flowers. They were pink and each carried a purple style tipped by a yellow stigma. Golden pollen was scattered all over them. Fertilisation had already taken place. But what had done it? A steady stream of tiny sweat bees were travelling in and out through the gap created by the collapsed pleats. They were certainly carrying pollen, packed in the baskets on their legs. Could they have done the work? Some botanists have suggested that the titan employs carrion beetles for the job. Certainly the smell of putrefaction

◁
The six-foot tall fruiting stem of the titan arum standing in the Sumatran forest. The crossed poles to the right are the cut stems of the giant leaves. A young leaf is sprouting in the background on the left

that the inflorescence is said to emit would suggest that. We, however, saw no sign of them.

Such a gigantic inflorescence seems unnecessarily large to attract
pollinators as small as sweat bees or even carrion beetles. However,
its size is more likely to be connected with the pungency and distribution of its odour than the size of its pollinators. Since an individual plant is only able to reproduce during two days of its
seven-year life, its need for pollinators as soon as its flower opens,
is urgent. If pollen is to be brought from another flower, then those
pollinators will have to come from a great distance, for as we had
discovered to our cost, the flowers are rare and widely dispersed.
To produce its perfume, the plant raises its internal temperature
several degrees above that of its surroundings and vaporises oils
secreted in its heart. The perfume then emerges from a slit in the
side of the spadix. It would be more accurate, therefore, to compare
the spadix with a factory chimney rather than a church spire, and
plainly the taller it is the more widely it will disperse its scent. And
it is indeed spectacularly successful in doing so, for the villagers
who had guided us to the flower told us that even they had discovered it by sniffing the air from fifty yards away.

◇

The titan arum may have the biggest of all flower-like structures,
but it certainly does not have the most complex or intimate of
relationships with its pollinating partners. That distinction must be
given to flowers so small that several hundred fit into a tiny green
ball the size of a marble, and so insignificant that they never even
see the light of day. These green spheres are inflorescences produced by tropical figs such as the African sycamore fig and they
grow in bunches directly from the fig's trunk. Each one has a small
hole on the surface opposite its stalk. This is the entrance to the
inflorescence and it is on this that the fig's insect partners alight.

They are tiny wasps only two millimetres long belonging to a
group known as the gall wasps. Members of this family inject their
eggs into the body of a plant, its leaf perhaps or its stem. The plant
so attacked reacts by developing a ball of tissue, a gall, around the

Little figs sprout directly from the trunk and branches of the sycamore fig. South-eastern Africa

wasp egg. When the grub hatches, it eats the gall from the inside, pupates in the little chamber it has created, and then flies away.

The gall wasp that lands on the fig's inflorescence is always a female. She has already mated and is needing to deposit her eggs. She begins to force her way into the tiny hole in the inflorescence. This is not easy for the entrance is guarded by overlapping scales. Sometimes her antennae are damaged in the process and she nearly always loses both her wings.

She has entered a small circular chamber lined with the fig's minuscule flowers. Those nearest the entrance are male, but they are not yet mature and have not started to produce their pollen. She crawls over those and goes deeper inside the chamber. There she finds the female flowers. They are flask-shaped and of two kinds, long-necked and short-necked. She now unpacks pollen that she has been carrying in special pouches on the sides of her abdomen and spreads it over the stigmas of the female flowers.

She has served the fig's purpose. Now she has to serve her own. She starts to lay her eggs by inserting her ovipositor into a stigma so that, like a hypodermic needle, it pierces the length of the style and reaches the little chamber which holds this particular flower's single egg. If she tries to do this with a long-necked flower, her ovipositor is unable to reach the egg chamber. So she withdraws it. When she inserts it into a short-necked flower, she has success.

The injection of her egg has the same effect on the plant as is usual in her family – the fig flower develops a tiny gall around the egg. Several females may have entered the inflorescence and several hundred female flowers will have been treated in this way. The female wasps then die. Their job is done.

The days pass. The eggs hatch. The young grubs, with the special food provided for them by the fig, develop very rapidly. But the different sexes do so at different speeds. First to emerge from the galls as adults are males. They are very odd-looking, blind, wingless and almost wormlike. As soon as one is free from his gall, he starts searching for females. He can detect just where they are, even though they have not yet emerged from their galls, and when he finds one, he starts to gnaw into the gall to reach her. As soon as he succeeds, he turns and mates with her.

The males have one further job to do. They assemble in a team and together start to gnaw a burrow through the inflorescence wall. The females, who have now emerged, could not do this for their jaws are not as big and as strong as those of the males. In any case, they might damage their wings in the process and they are going to need them.

While the males are working at the tunnel, their sisters are moving around within the chamber, crawling over the male fig-flowers. These have now matured and are discharging their pollen. The young female wasps load it into their pouches. They themselves will not benefit from this act, but the fig will. And so, therefore, will their offspring – eventually.

At last the males finish their labours. The tunnel is complete and the way is clear to the outside world. But the males who dug it cannot take advantage of it. With neither wings nor eyes, they would be helpless outside. They die where they were born, inside the fig's inflorescence. But the young females clamber through it and fly away, carrying the fig's pollen with them, to seek new fig inflorescences and start the whole cycle over again.

But they are not the only insects to emerge from the fig. Just as there are bees which cheat by collecting nectar from a flower with-

▷
The sectioned fruit of a sycamore fig. A female of one of the wasp-cheats has just emerged from her cell, complete with wings and immensely long ovipositor

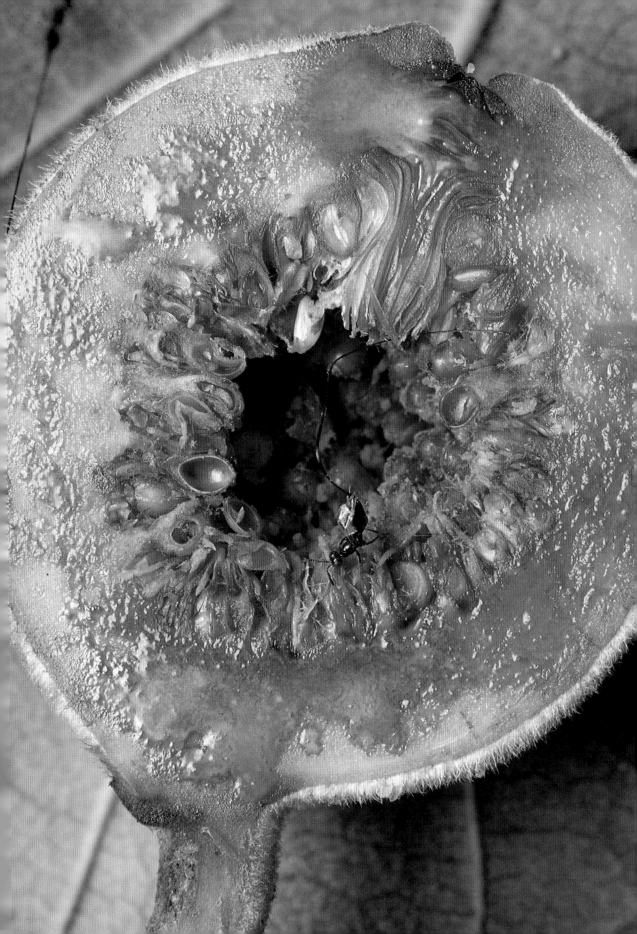

out pollinating it, so there are fig wasps which cheat when using the fig's flower chamber as a nursery. The female wasp of this species has an enormously long ovipositor which she inserts into the fig, so that she is able to lay her eggs inside without ever entering it and pollinating the flowers.

It is plain, in view of all the complex arrangements made by plants, that cross-fertilisation is very important to them. That being so, precautions must be taken to prevent a flower from fertilising itself. In some plants, this cannot happen, for male flowers are carried on different individuals from female flowers. In those where stamens and style are in the same flower, there may be a biochemical block. The stigma on the tip of the style recognises pollen from its own plant and does not respond to it chemically so that it does not develop. Sometimes, as in the arums, the male organs do not mature and produce pollen until the female organs have either been fertilised by pollen from another individual or ceased to be receptive. The common English primrose prevents self-fertilisation by having two kinds of flowers, the pin-eyed and the thrum-eyed. The pin-eyed flower has a long style that rises high in its throat, and stamens are attached half-way down it. The thrum-eyed flower has them placed exactly the other way round, with stamens near the top of its throat and a stigma on a very short style near the bottom. The consequence of this arrangement is that a pollinating insect visiting a short-styled, high-stamened flower, delving deep to reach the nectar, only collects pollen around the end of its abdomen. If it visits another of the same kind this pollen will not reach the short style. If, however, it seeks nectar from a long-styled flower, then that pollen will be brushed neatly onto the stigma. Equally pollen from a long-styled flower will only collect on the insect's head and reach the stigma of a short-styled one. So cross-fertilisation is assured.

The importance of cross-fertilisation is usually said to be that it ensures a shuffling of an individual's genes. As a result, small physical variations will appear in the next generation, and these are the raw material upon which evolution works. In recent years, some have thought this explanation a little pat and a little vague. The idea has been put forward that such variation is primarily necessary to keep ahead of disease-causing bacteria which are themselves continually and very rapidly evolving and producing new variants

▷
The primrose's insurance against self-pollination is to grow in two forms – pin-eyed with a long stigma (right) and thrum-eyed (left) with a short stigma and protruding stamens

▷
The pin- and thrum-eyed primrose flowers in section

◁
The British bee orchid, bereft of a regular insect partner, has to rely on self-pollination

with new abilities to overwhelm a plant's defences. This, however, is still a contentious view.

Yet in spite of all their complex techniques, the imprisonments and inveiglings, the bribes and flirtations, plants do not always succeed in transferring grains of pollen from one individual to another. Sometimes the wind simply does not blow in the right direction at the right time. Sometimes the appropriate insect does not find the flower. And sometimes the insect-plant partnership is irretrievably broken.

Britain has an orchid, closely related and very similar to the European mirror orchid. This is the bee orchid and its lip certainly does look like a brown rather hairy bee. But male bees rarely if ever land on it. No one knows for sure why this should be. Perhaps its true insect partner was a species that was driven out of Britain when the country froze during the Ice Age. Nevertheless, the orchid still manages to set seed. A day or so after a flower opens, its pollinia fall out of the anthers and hang down in front of the stigma. The wind shaking the flower is then quite sufficient to cause the pollinia to brush against the stigma and stick to it. Cross-fertilisation has been denied it, but the orchid has banished its previous inhibitions and accepts its own pollen.

Other plants that have simply been unfortunate in one particular season and failed to find a pollinator also have similar fail-safe mechanisms. The foxglove, at the end of the flowering season sheds its whole floral tube. The stamens along the lower part of their length are fused to it, so they come away too. In the process, they brush past the long stigma. If an insect hasn't provided it with pollen, they do.

But some plants, if conditions for pollination are not suitable, respond in a more radical and energy-saving way. Dog violets produce flowers which in the spring are pollinated by bees and butterflies. But later, in summer there are much fewer such insects around. So the violet does not open such late flower buds. Packed within them are all the structural elements of a flower, fully formed, except that they are smaller and there are fewer of them. The petals are only about half the size of those produced earlier in the season, and there are only two stamens instead of five. But they produce enough pollen to react with the nearby stigma. The seeds that then develop are nonetheless fertile.

Cross-pollination may be the ideal; great efforts and stratagems are made in order to achieve it; but its failure need not necessarily result in the total extinction of the genetic line of an annual plant or the waste of a yearly opportunity of a longer-lived one. If arrangements are made for self-pollination, then although the next generation will be genetically identical, at least a next generation will appear and they, when they bloom, may be luckier.

4

THE SOCIAL
STRUGGLE

LAND THAT HAS nutritious well-watered soil and reasonable temperatures will, in the normal course of events, be dominated by trees. Their height enables them to intercept the all-important light before it reaches smaller rivals, and their extensive network of roots extracts most of the available water. Other plants, if they are to live in such environments, have to adjust their requirements to match what remains when the trees have taken all they need. But on occasion, even long-established forests lose their hold on the land.

A great hurricane struck Britain on the night of October 16th, 1987. It had been raining heavily that day but even professional forecasters did not foresee the ferocity of the storm that was brewing out at sea in the Bay of Biscay. It was moving in a north-easterly direction. In the early hours of the morning, it crossed the south coast of England. Winds rose to over a hundred miles an hour, overturning lorries, blowing down chimney stacks, lifting roofs and felling church spires. As it moved into woodlands, it uprooted oaks that had stood for four hundred years. Great beeches with trunks yards across snapped like matchsticks. In plantations, younger trees were felled in great swathes, as though they had been scythed. Had southern England been in its primeval state, its blanket of oak forest would have been devastated, even though trees in continuous closed woodlands are less vulnerable to damage than those standing in isolation. As it was, in those few hours, over fifteen million trees were destroyed.

For mature trees, of course, the night was a catastrophe. But for other woodland plants, lying as seeds in the soil, undecayed and still viable, it was the opportunity for which they had been waiting for decades. A few months later, as the weather warmed, photo-

◁

A plantation of trees in Kent felled by the 1987 hurricane

△
Foxgloves carpet a sunlit clearing created by a fallen tree in the New Forest, Hampshire

sensitive substances in their coats registered the increased light that fell on them and the embryonic plants within responded. Around the fallen trees, the ground became dotted with foxglove seedlings.

Foxgloves must have good light if they are to grow. The 1987 hurricane gave the species in southern England its greatest opportunity of the century. But every year there are isolated tree-falls in the woodlands and a chance for a few foxgloves to move into new territory. They develop very swiftly, for woodland soil is extremely nutritious, having been enriched over many years by rotting leaves. With the death of a tree, these nutrients are available to others and the young foxgloves are quick to claim them. The seedlings rapidly grow rosettes of large leaves. Soon, in the sunshine, they are manufacturing food in such quantity that they have more than they currently need and they store the surplus in their swollen roots.

In their first year, they develop no further, but the following spring, the clearing still being open to the sky, they continue to grow in size and build up their food store. Then as their second summer approaches, they use their reserves to send up tall spikes of handsome purple flowers. A few months later still, each spike releases about a quarter of a million seeds which are carried away by the wind. Some of the plants may survive for another year or so, but many now die. They have had their opportunity. The vast majority of their offspring will not be so fortunate. Even the luckiest among them may have to wait further decades before they can come to life and even then they will only find that opportunity in another place.

The foxgloves do not have their newly-acquired territory to themselves for long. Nettles also require nutrient-rich soil and they too compete for a place in the clearings They are slower to get started but once they have done so they spread rapidly in a way that the foxgloves are unable to match. They develop horizontal underground stems that form such a closely tangled mat that few other seeds are able to grow among them. As time passes, they grow so tall that they are easily knocked over by a passing animal and may even bend down under their own weight. But that is far from a disaster. Wherever their stems touch the ground, they put down fresh roots and send up new stems. So they swiftly expand their territory and develop into a dense patch. Unlike the foxgloves, they do not die after two years or so but continue to flourish, especially if the ground happens to have been enriched with phosphates from the dung of forest animals. Human beings, one way and another, also deposit a lot of phosphate around their dwellings. It comes not only from their middens, but from the ash of the wood they burn, from the bones of the animals they eat, and from their own bodies. So an isolated patch of nettles in a wood is strong evidence that the site was once cleared of its trees and was probably occupied by people.

Within a few years, these initial colonisers of forest clearings have extracted so much of the nutriment from the soil that it can no longer meet all their needs and they begin to falter. The seeds of other plants, better provisioned with larger food stores, are also competitors in this race. They started more slowly but now they begin to catch up as the early sprinters become exhausted. Birch are among them. Their seeds are small and light enough to be transported by the wind and they are produced in large numbers. These too will

⊲
*Birch seedlings
growing after a
forest fire*

only germinate in open well-lit positions. They also require the long
days of summer and unless they receive sixteen hours of light in
twenty-four, they will not sprout. Having sprouted, they then have
the ability to remain as seedlings without growing significantly any
further for several years until the conditions begin to favour them.

Eventually, young birch saplings begin to rise above the other
plants in the clearing, sometimes growing in such numbers that they
form a thicket. As time passes, the more vigorous among them begin
to overtop the others and the thicket thins out. The ground beneath
them is now shaded by their leafy branches during the summer and
the smaller light-loving plants growing there can survive no longer.
The land has become a birch wood.

But not even the birches are likely to be the long-term holders of
this territory. When the clearings were first created by tree falls, jays
and squirrels planted them with acorns. They gathered them from
the surrounding woodland in the autumn and buried them to serve
as food stores during the hard months of winter. But some were
forgotten and they will have sprouted. There are not likely to be
many of them, but their chances of survival are good. Acorns carry

△
*A jay takes an
acorn from its
winter storage*

very large stores of food, far bigger than those of birch seeds and
they sustain the oak seedlings through their difficult first months.
The young oaks grow slowly. The demands they make on the soil
are less than those of the swift-growing birch. But each year they
are bigger and stronger and eventually the time comes when they
begin to rival the birches. In this long race, the tortoise is beginning
to catch up with the hare.

The birches, in any case, are beginning to fail. They are not long-
lived trees even in the most favourable uncontested circumstances
and seldom live longer than fifty or sixty years. So it is that, ultimately, the oaks reclaim the territory they lost decades earlier.

◇

*England's natural
mantle, a mature
oak woodland*
▷ ▷

A mature oak tree, standing a hundred feet tall, provides lodging,
and often board as well, for more different kinds of animals than
any other European tree. Thirty species of birds, forty-five different
bugs and over two hundred species of moth have been collected
from oaks. Each part of the tree has its own particular lodgers.

Chafers and click-beetle larvae live in the roots. Tiny moths, many with wingspans of less than an inch, conceal themselves in crevices of the bark during the day and fly around the branches at night. Immediately beneath the bark, beetles burrow away, excavating tiny radiating galleries and borer beetles drill their shafts into the wood.

The leaves, soft and succulent, are eaten by adult cockchafer beetles and by the caterpillars of many different species of moth. The bigger ones chew their way stolidly through them. The smaller ones mine tunnels within the thickness of the leaf blade and content themselves with the softer tissues they find there. A weevil, the red oak roller, uses a leaf as a container for its young. It cuts the leaf transversely across the middle to the central rib, working first from one side then the other. It folds together the two quarters nearer the tip over the midrib and then rolls them into a double thickness tube. In that it lays its eggs.

Many leaves carry curious lumps, swellings and spheres. The variety of these galls is indicated by the names foresters give them – red pea, cherry, marble, oyster, silk button, spangle, and biggest of all, apple. These are the result of activities of a great variety of small creatures – midges, moths, worms, and most numerous of all, tiny wasps less than an eighth of an inch long. They all lay their eggs either within leaves or leaf buds and the oak tree reacts by producing an abnormal growth around them. The substance of this provides the young developing inside with food. Often, the grubs stay inside the gall even after the leaf falls and do not burrow their way out of it as adults until the following spring. Smaller galls contain just one single larva but a big gall such as an oak apple may contain up to thirty.

The oak's acorns, so rich in nutriment, provide meals for another whole range of diners. There is a lot for them to feed on, for a mature oak may produce 90,000 acorns a year – several million in its lifetime. Since only one acorn from each tree need grow to maturity each century to maintain the oak population, there is a vast surplus. Animals of all kinds make sure that it is not wasted. Rooks and jays rip the acorns from the branches as they mature. Wood pigeons are particularly gluttonous. One of them can hold seventy in its crop at any one time and consume a hundred and twenty in a day. Weevils

◁

A male oak roller beetle (top) stands on guard while the female prepares to flex an oak leaf

▷

Having severed the blade of the leaf, the female begins to fold it before rolling

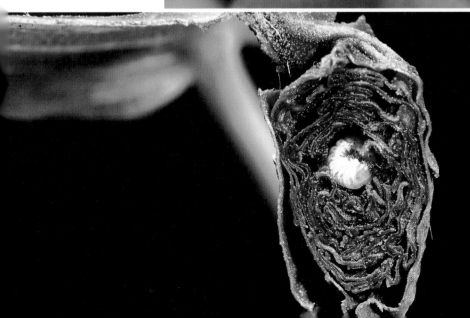

◁

The finished construction, halved to reveal the larva developing within

bore holes into them with their long snouts and lay their eggs there. And when those acorns that survive this toll fall to the ground, they are greedily collected by mice, squirrels, deer and, in mainland Europe, by wild pig.

The consumers of the oak's tissues, in their turn, serve as food for another set of animals. Wasps, spiders and ladybird larvae hunt for the caterpillars. Native birds are now beginning to nest and the females need to feed intensively in order to produce their eggs. Spotted woodpeckers and tree creepers clamber over the oak's bark, picking out insects hidden in the crevices. Great tits time the production of their families to coincide with that when the caterpillars are most abundant on the oak leaves and a parent bird, with nestlings to feed, may collect at least three hundred caterpillars a day. Many migrants including warblers and nightingales fly up to Britain from warmer parts of Europe to share in the feast. And these small birds themselves become the food of bigger birds – magpies and jays – which take not only eggs and nestlings but the adults of smaller species. As the oak ages and holes develop in its trunk, owls and bats may take up residence inside it; and down among its gnarled interlacing roots, badgers and foxes burrow out their homes.

Oaks are indeed the lords of the forest, and in the proper traditions of reigning monarchs, they provide a livelihood for a multitude of the smaller inhabitants of their kingdom.

◇

The rich pastures of the summer woodlands in northern countries are not all permanent. As autumn approaches the days grow colder. The visiting birds begin to fly back southwards. A few butterflies and moths, having deposited their eggs in safe places, may find crevices in which to hibernate, but most of them die. And the oaks, together with beeches, birches and other broad-leaved trees, shed their delicate frost-vulnerable leaves. Their life processes slow down and their growth comes almost to a halt.

With the disappearance of their leaf canopy, the oaks have temporarily lost the dominance of their territory. For the first time in many months the pale winter sunshine reaches the forest floor. But few plants there can make use of it at this time. Most, like the oaks, have lost their leaves and suspended their activities.

Eventually, the year turns. Every day the sun rises slightly higher in the sky. At last the time comes when the ground beneath the leafless branches warms sufficiently for plants to grow. A whole group of them are prepared for this moment and are ready to spring into life. A year ago, during the previous spring, they had synthesised food and stored it underground in their bulbs. Now they will spend those reserves. Only the slightest rise in temperature is necessary to trigger their activity. The snowdrop, as its name suggests, may appear even before the winter snow has totally left the ground. Shortly afterwards, primroses put out their leaves. Even though they lack bulbs, they photosynthesise so effectively that soon their lovely yellow flowers appear. Then, as the buds begin to burst on the branches of the trees above, the bluebells rise from their bulbs and sheets of blue spread across the woodland floor.

Bluebells carpeting an English woodland in spring
▽

The North American spring brings similar glories. In the Appalachian Mountains of Virginia and North Carolina, during April, the woods are knee-deep in white trillium lilies and blue delphiniums. Spring flowers are even more varied here than they are in Europe. In an English woodland, you may find two or three different species of flower in a square yard; in the Appalachians you can discover a dozen or more.

But this glorious richness does not last for long, either in Europe or in North America. The sap begins to rise in the trunks of the trees and the young leaves burst from their buds and spread in the sunshine. Below, the shade returns. The spring flowers have passed their peak. The leaves of some, lacking sufficient light to operate efficiently, shrivel and die. By late spring many of the ground plants have lapsed back into dormancy. The trees have reconstructed their canopy and reclaimed the light.

◇

The wooden pillars and struts, the girders and trellises with which the trees support their light-gathering screens of leaves can equally

△
Trillium lilies at the beginning of their flowering season in the woods of New England. As they age, so they turn first pink and then red

well support the leaves of others. Many plants have developed ways of clambering up trees to use their branches for that purpose.

Almost every element of plant anatomy, it seems, can be turned into some kind of climbing device. The cheese plant climbs with its roots, sending them out from its nodes, the places on its stem from which leaves normally spring, and wrapping them around the trunk of its host. European ivy sprouts roots all along the underside of its stems. They are so thin that they can cling to any tiny rugosity. Honeysuckle uses its own stem, winding it around the thicker stem of others. The glory lilies of tropical Africa and Asia have elongated the tips of their leaves into little mobile wires with which they hook themselves on to any support they can find.

Vetches and passion flowers have modified some of their leaves even more extremely and converted them into tendrils. These grope

▷
The glory lily climbs with the aid of tendrils formed from the elongated midribs of its leaves

around in space until they touch the stem of another and swiftly coil around it. The tendrils of Virginia creeper end in small adhesive pads which stick firmly to stone or bark.

◁
The end of a honeysuckle's stem serves as a tendril with which the plant searches for a hold on a neighbour

Tendrils can be extremely sensitive. Those of a species of gourd will react even if the stimulus is only a thread of wool drawn across their surface. Furthermore, if the support contacted by a tendril is extremely smooth and unlikely to provide the kind of roughness needed for a secure grip, the tendril will unwind and resume its blind search. Once having found what suits it and established a firm hold, it begins to coil its middle section into the shape of a spring. This shortens its overall length and pulls it closer to the plant it has grasped so that other shoots can the more easily attach themselves to it.

Rattans, the highly specialised climbing palms of south-east Asia, have stems that are barely thicker than a man's finger. The front tip, from which all growth comes, explores with extremely long, thin tendrils equipped along their length with needle-sharp curved hooks. If these snag your arm – and the tendrils are so thin that they can easily be overlooked – they can rip both your shirt and your flesh. With these, it hitches itself on to an established tree and actively grows upwards. Sometimes the support is not strong enough to bear the extra load and it collapses, but the rattan is not

The thin barbed stem of a rattan palm reaches upwards seeking for support

deterred. It continues to grow as it sprawls across the forest floor and does so with such vigour that some species develop longer stems than any other plant and may reach a length of over five hundred feet.

◁
*Once established, a
rattan climbs up
through the
branches of its
supporting tree
until it emerges
above the canopy to
bask in the sunshine*

Some of these climbers use their grasping devices to ascend mature trees. Others, more deviously, hitch themselves on to a sapling tree and climb upwards on to higher branches as the young tree produces them, so that even when the supporting tree is mature and has discarded the branches from the lower part of its now pillar-like trunk, there is nonetheless a climber dangling from its crown.

Most big trees in the rain forests of the tropics bear these burdens. Only one kind is usually immune. Palm trees, with very few exceptions, do not branch. They generate all their growth from the huge bud at their apex, the so-called palm-heart. This produces leaf after leaf as the trunk grows taller and taller. The great leaves, after some time, die and are shed. As they fall, they take with them any climber that has managed to attach itself. So palm trunks are nearly always free and clean.

*The branch of a
giant tree in the
cloud forest of
Brazil, loaded with
epiphytes*
▽

There is yet another way by which smaller plants can reach the brightly-lit haven of the forest canopy. They can travel up there as seeds. Some, such as those of orchids, are so small that they are wafted up by the gentlest breeze. Others, having been swallowed

for the sake of their succulent coatings, are deposited there in the droppings of fruit-eating monkeys or birds.

So successful are these techniques for sending seeds up into the canopy that the massive branches of many forest trees are often densely lined with squatters. These are known as epiphytes and among the commonest of them are bromeliads. They anchor themselves by wrapping their roots around the branch. Their long leaves grow in a tight rosette around their central bud and channel rain water down to it so that the rosette fills and forms a small pond. This becomes a world in miniature. Leaves and other bits of vegetable detritus fall into it and decay. Birds and small mammals come to sip the water, and leave behind their nitrogen-rich droppings. Microscopic organisms of one kind or another develop in it, as they will do in any pool of standing water. Mosquitos lay rafts of eggs that float on the surface. Dragonflies deposit their eggs in its depths, though in much smaller numbers. In due course, a few dragonfly larvae will feed on a multitude of mosquito larvae. Small brilliantly coloured frogs that live nowhere else but in bromeliad ponds take up residence and spawn there. Crabs, salamanders, slugs, worms, beetles, lizards, even small snakes may all join the community.

The bromeliad benefits from its hospitality. The water in its pond turns brown with the products of decay. The droppings of its lodgers accumulate as a thick ooze in the bottom. From both the plant extracts valuable nutrients that it can find in no other way, perched as it is so far away from the soil which nourishes others.

Orchids of many kinds have also adopted this high life. They lack the ponds that sustain the bromeliads, so they must collect their nourishment in other ways. Some dangle their roots in the air, absorbing moisture from the humid atmosphere and rely on the tiny amount of nutriments it might have dissolved on its descent through the forest vegetation. Others spread their roots over the surface of the branches and collect the water that has trickled through the leaves and dripped from branch to branch, gathering a little nutriment on the way.

One orchid, taeniophyllum, has roots that are even more versatile. Its scientific name means, rather unattractively, "tapeworm leaf". Its roots have not only developed into flat, tapeworm-like shapes several yards long that writhe statically all over the branch on which

▷
Two of the many and varied inhabitants of the world within the heart of a bromeliad – a tiny arrow poison frog and a turbellarian worm

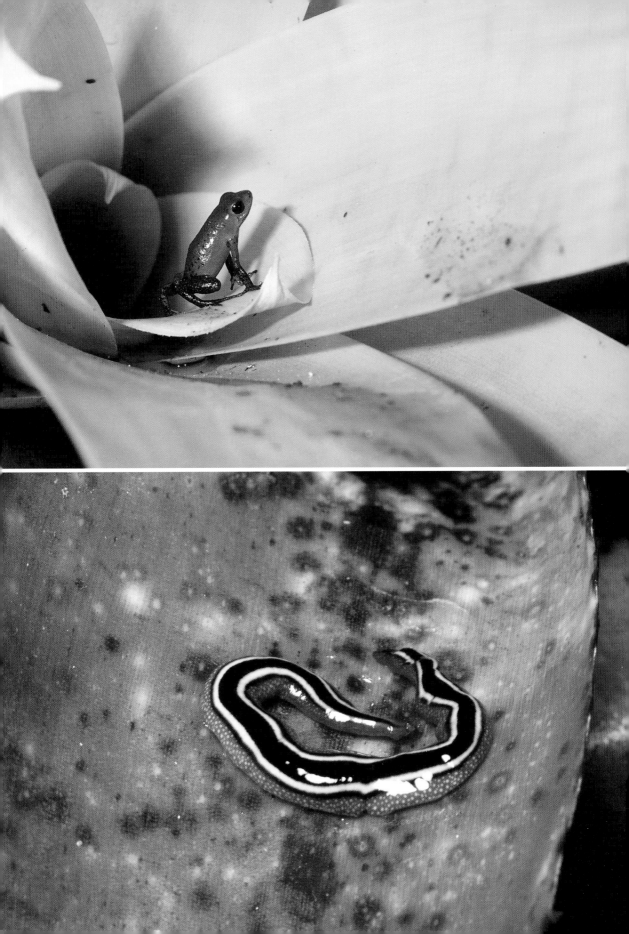

◁ *A bromeliad seedling, in spite of the sluicing rain, has managed to find a hold on the surface of a leaf. Brazil*

the plant sits, but they have also become green and manufacture the orchid's food. The true leaves, no longer needed, have been reduced to tiny scales on the minute stem that carries the flowers.

Some plants – particularly mosses and liverworts – will even take up residence on the surface of a forest tree's leaves. They are capable of growing so extensively and thickly that they significantly reduce the amount of light reaching the leaf. It is therefore greatly to the tree's advantage to get rid of them. Some trees do so by regularly shedding the waxy coat to their leaves. Others reduce the chance of the squatters getting a hold in the first place with the drip-tip at the far end of their leaves. This not only prevents rainwater from lingering on their surface, choking the pores and interfering with the process of photosynthesis, but by sluicing it swiftly away, clears off any spores or seeds.

◇

Orchids and bromeliads do little harm to a tree, except that sometimes they cause a branch to break because of their sheer weight. But among the squatters grow more sinister, and ultimately murderous plants. They are figs. To start with, they seem no more dangerous than the other epiphytes among which they grow, for they draw their sustenance from the vegetable debris that

▷ *The descending roots of a strangler fig encircle the trunk of its host in what will become a fatal embrace. Northern Australia*

accumulates around their roots entwining the branch. At this early stage in their lives they grow quite slowly. But gradually their roots extend along the branch and surround the main trunk. As they develop downwards they fuse into a kind of lattice. Others hang free and descend vertically. Once the roots reach the forest floor the fig is able to draw nutrients from the soil and so to grow with increased vigour. It embraces the trunk of its host with more and more roots and appears to be strangling it. It is certainly the case that broad-leaved trees grow by increasing their girth and that the embrace of the fig appears to prevent that, but it is more likely that the fig cripples its host by starvation rather than strangulation, for its bushy branches in the canopy collect most of the light and its roots around the base of the tree claim a major part of the soil's nutrients. In any event, before long, the host tree dies. But the fig itself does not fall to the ground. Although the trunk of its host rots away, the lattice of roots around the trunk is now so complete that they form a hollow cylinder and the former strangler remains standing upright without a victim. So the fig has become an independent forest giant with its own place in the canopy.

Sometimes a tree acquires several young figs on its branches. As they grow, their roots entwine with one another and become so enmeshed that when between them they have killed their host and stand independently, they appear to be a single individual. Researchers working in the forests of Panama started to take the genetic fingerprints of different branches of giant figs and they discovered that the majority of these trees consisted of two or three merged individuals. One proved to contain eight. This may explain something that has puzzled naturalists for a long time. Mature strangler figs often have branches that come into flower at different times of the year. This may be because such branches belong to different individuals with different fruiting cycles. It certainly makes strangler figs particularly valuable members of the forest community as far as fruit-eating animals are concerned, for a giant strangler that is an amalgam of several individuals can be a supermarket that produces a supply of food for much of the year.

◇

▷
With its host dead and rotted away, the roots of the strangler fig form a hollow latticed tower that stands independently. Indonesia

Eventually even the biggest and most vigorous of trees must fall. Its body will contain several tons of carbon, nitrogen, phosphorous and other valuable elements that the tree over its lifetime, has extracted from the atmosphere and the ground. But in this form these valuable substances are locked away and beyond the reach of any other plant or animal, for the cellulose and lignin, which make up most of the bulk of a tree are extraordinarily stable substances. No animal digestion can break them down. No plant root can dissolve them. Only two kinds of living things can reduce them to their basic elements – bacteria and fungi.

Fungi are very strange organisms. They have no stems, roots or leaves. Even the most advanced and complex of them are nothing more, for most of the time, than an interwoven tissue of branching threads. At first sight, they might seem to be simple plants, rather like algae that for some reason have lost their chlorophyll and therefore can only feed on the tissues of other plants or animals, living or dead. Indeed, early naturalists considered them to be exactly that, which is why fungi are still regarded as being within the province of botany. But they are fundamentally different from plants. Their cell walls are composed not of cellulose, as is the case with all plants, but chitin, the material from which insects construct their hard external skeletons. Yet it makes no sense to classify them with animals either. We now know that their cells divide in a way that is so fundamentally different from any other organism that it sets them apart from both animals and plants. Fungi constitute a kingdom that is entirely their own.

They exist throughout a wood or a forest but they are, most of the time invisible, for they are hidden in the soil. We only become aware of them when, seemingly almost overnight, mushrooms and toadstools rise from the ground and stand, for a few days, in clumps at the base of a tree, in wide rings in a clearing, or in lines along a rotting trunk. These are fruiting bodies, the fungal equivalent of flowers. The parallel must not be drawn too closely, for the genetic particles produced by these structures are not seeds but spores. They are microscopically small, for they consist of no more than a single cell and they carry no food store to sustain the young individual that will emerge from them. Nor does one need to fuse with another in order to grow. They are fertile in themselves. The fruiting

▷
Fungi, the only organisms apart from bacteria that can digest wood, feed on the fallen trunk of a rain forest tree, releasing the nutrients it contains. Northern Australia

bodies of fungi, therefore, do not have to attract pollinators of any kind, as the flowers of plants must do. Their function is solely one of distribution.

Spores are so small that they are easily carried away by the slightest breeze, but even so, they have to be released in such a way that the wind can catch them. Mushrooms and toadstools, with their heads lifted several inches above the ground, simply shed their spores from the vertical plates on their underside, their so-called gills. A single mushroom, in the few days before it decays, may discharge ten thousand million of them.

Another whole section of the fungal kingdom produces its spores in tiny tubes. As these structures mature, they change chemically so that they begin to absorb water and they do so with such vigour that the tube bursts, usually at the tip. A cap is thrown off or a lid cast back and the spores shoot out. In some species they may travel a foot or so. That may not seem far, but it can be crucial. One such fungus grows on cowpats. Its method of distribution requires that it should be eaten by a grazing animal and eventually, after the animal has moved elsewhere, emerge with its dung. For that to happen the spores must land on something that its host is about to eat. And that is not a cowpat. The range of its little guns may not be spectacularly long but it is usually enough to carry the spores over the dung surrounding it and deposit them on the surrounding grass.

Many puffballs project their spores vertically into the air. As they mature, they become hollow and shed their spores internally. The walls of the ball harden and become so rigid that the slightest knock, or even the impact of a rain drop causes it to vibrate and the spores are ejected out of a hole in the top, like a cloud of smoke. Others, including the giant European puffball that may be eighteen inches across, collapse the whole of their upper half and the wind then blows the fragments around. The number of spores produced by such a monster is said to be up to seven and a half million. Someone has calculated that were each of these to grow to maturity, and then in turn produce fruiting bodies, the potential mass of their offspring would be eight hundred times the volume of the earth.

The tiny bird's nest fungus produces a little saucer in which nestle a few small "eggs". The clutch size varies from a couple to eight or

▷
The giant puffball of Europe and North America can grow to a weight of 30 pounds and a diameter of 18 inches.

ten. Each is a small capsule filled with spores and each is attached to the saucer by a thin filament. The saucer is so shaped that if a heavy raindrop falls in it, water droplets are deflected up around the sides, detaching the capsules and projecting them for a distance of up to six feet. Their attaching threads unwind behind them and finally break. They have a sticky end so that as the capsule shoots through surrounding vegetation, the filament catches on a leaf or a stem and the capsule hangs there. Then when conditions are just right, it releases its spores.

The 'eggs' of a bird's nest fungus will be bounced out of the 'nest' by raindrops

The fungi belonging to the group known as earth-stars produce a ball with a double skin. When this ripens, the outer skin splits and turns inside out, so pushing the inner sphere upwards. The under surface of the split skin, in some species, is brightly coloured, red or yellow, so that an earth-star at this stage looks almost flower-like. The spores then puff out from a hole in the centre of the inner bag.

Stink-horns use insects as distributors. When they first push up through the ground, they look like eggs, but soon a spike, capped with a slimy brown head breaks through the skin of the egg and grows upwards with astonishing speed. In many tropical species, the spike carries a long lacy skirt. This strange phallic apparition

△
*A lacy stinkhorn
fungus from the
rain forest of Peru*

gives off a lavatorial smell that is as unpleasant to our nostrils as it is attractive to flies. They settle on the brown slime and feed on the sugars that it contains. Like insects collecting pollen from a flower, they inevitably become dusted with spores and these they carry away with them.

Perhaps most remarkable of all these fruiting bodies are the luminous mushrooms of the tropics. It may well be that their greenish lights, glowing on the forest floor at night, serve to attract animal messengers, but just what they are is still not known.

With the aid of such devices, fungi, in the form of spores, pervade the world. Over a hundred thousand different species of them have been named and there are probably twice as many still awaiting scientific identification. They sail high in the sky. They float in rivers and in the sea. They can live in conditions where there is no oxygen, and tolerate temperatures as high as 140 degrees Fahrenheit and as low as 6 degrees below freezing. An acre of meadowland may contain about 2,500 pounds of them, about the same in weight as twenty five sheep. A few, like yeasts, smuts and rusts remain as single cells, but most exist as threads that branch, fuse and interweave and so form mats, tangled tissues or long root-like strings. The honey-fungus, which attacks the roots of trees and produces

◁

The variety of forms assumed by the fruiting bodies of fungi is huge. These come from Tasmania (top left), Kenya (top right), Brazil (bottom left) and Western Europe (bottom right)

yellow-brown mushrooms, has a claim to be the biggest of all living organisms. Researchers working in the forests of Michigan in the United States discovered that threads of it, taken over an area of 150,000 square yards – about 40 acres – were all genetically identical. All therefore had to be reckoned as being interconnected parts of a single individual which was probably at least 1,500 years old.

The variety of substances that fungi can digest is extraordinary. Some can live on petroleum, others on the thin films that coat lenses. Silica, magnesium, iron, even plastic are all consumed by one kind or another. At least fifty species are active hunters, albeit on a microscopic scale. They develop little hoops on the side of their threads which carry three sensitive pads on their inner margin. These hoops produce a chemical smell which attracts tiny eel-worms. If one wriggles into the ring, the pads suddenly swell and the worm is gripped so tightly, it cannot escape. Filaments from the ring then grow into the worm and suck out the contents of its body.

▷

A thread of fungus captures an eel-worm

In forests, fungi feed predominantly on dead plant tissue. Great quantities of it lie on the ground and all of it is at their disposal since no other kind of organism can digest it. They attack it with a powerful acid. The fact that their own bodies are constructed from chitin is clearly very significant. Were they made of cellulose, they would be in danger of dissolving themselves.

In the warm humid atmosphere of the tropical rain forest,the fungi work fast. The nutrients they release filter down into the soil and as they do so, they are absorbed by the tree through a mass of tiny rootlets growing within an inch or so of the soil surface and often extending upwards into the leaf litter itself. Since there is little wind in a forest, the leaves are likely to have fallen directly down-wards, so a tree is usually able to reclaim much of what was once its own. But it has to work fast before the frequent rains wash away the nutrients and carry them within reach of other plants.

In cooler, more temperate woods, fungal decay is somewhat less swift and vegetable debris builds up to form a layer that moulders away more slowly and forms one of the richest of soils. Nutritious though it may be, seedlings germinating there may nonetheless face severe problems. In the coniferous forests of the north-west coast of America, the trees – Sitka spruce, hemlock and Douglas fir – may grow over two hundred feet high and they cut out most of the light. There is enough, however, to sustain ferns and other shade-loving plants, and the soil is so rich that they form a dense ground-cover through which you wade waist high. But beneath them, on the surface of the soil, it is very dark indeed. Seedlings, even if they were able to germinate, would not be able to gather enough light for them to photosynthesise. How then, can the giant trees regener-ate themselves?

They do so with the aid of their own dead bodies. The girth of an adult tree is such that the upper side of a fallen trunk remains above the ferns. A seed from a neighbouring tree that lands on it can thus get sufficient light to germinate. Being perched there brings another advantage: the bark of the prostrate tree is very fibrous and holds moisture like a sponge so the young plant does not lack for water. As the seedling sprouts, it sends down roots. They grow over the flank of the log and down into the rich soil beneath. As they gain strength, these roots thicken. While they are doing so, fungi are feasting in the wood of the log. Slowly it rots and begins to crumble away providing more sustenance for the young trees. After several decades, the log has been reduced to mouldering fragments. But the young seedlings still hold their position high above the ferns for their roots have now become so thick, they support them like stilts.

△
*Conifer seeds,
sprouting on the
top of a fallen log
above the shade of
the ground plants,
are able to grow
vigorously*

Inevitably, many of these young seedlings will not survive, but even after the years have reduced their numbers, there may be a dozen or so standing in a line above the remains of the log that nursed them. A century later, that number may be reduced to perhaps six or seven, but even so, they form a dramatic feature in the forest – half a dozen giants all of the same age, all standing on stilts and all in a line of almost military straightness. It is even possible sometimes to crawl down the tunnel made by their arching roots to trace the course and measure the length of the nurse-log to which they owe their lives.

The problem posed to tree seedlings by thick ground cover is greater still in the mountain ash forests of southern Australia. Here, the understorey is considerably higher for it is dominated by tree

ferns which stand ten feet tall. Even the stoutest trunk of a giant eucalypt, when fallen, cannot provide a platform above their fronds. The mountain ash seedlings, if they are to survive, need even more dramatic help than a tree-fall. They must have fire.

Bush fires burn every year in Australia, to a greater or lesser degree, but that which started in the state of Victoria in 1983 was to be one of the greatest catastrophes of the century for the human inhabitants. February 16th was, by bitter coincidence, Ash Wednesday. The whole country was suffering from a severe drought. In some parts, no rain had fallen for five years. The bush was tinder dry. Everyone was alert to the danger of fire. But fires are not always started by the carelessness of human beings. At least a fifth of those that burn every season in Victoria have a non-human origin. One of the commonest causes is lightning. It may strike a tall tree and cut a deep groove that zig-zags down the bark of its trunk as the bolt flashes down to earth. Sometimes such strikes are accompanied by torrential rain that can douse any fire. But not always.

What started fires that day is still not known. The weather was particularly hot – around 110 degrees Fahrenheit. There was a wind blowing at 40 miles an hour from the south-west. Perhaps a power-line snapped and electricity sparked to earth, setting the bush alight. Whatever the reason, people living in small towns in the north of the state saw the horizon darken as though with storm clouds. It was not rain. It was smoke. Soon they could smell the fire and hear its roar. Before long, they could see flames leaping high into the sky. The fire was advancing towards them faster than a man could run. The great trees in the bush were engulfed by flames and consumed so swiftly that they exploded with noises like rifle shots. As the blaze intensified it became a fire-storm. The heat sucked in so much air from all sides that a vortex developed in the sky above the fire, like the funnel of a tornado, except that here the threatening twisting column was made not of dust but flames. They rose sixty feet from the ground. Above them, balls of fire, composed of burning volatile gases given off by the incinerating gum trees, flared through the sky and sailed ahead, setting light to bush as much as three miles in front of the main fire.

There was nothing now that any fire brigade could do to stem the disaster. By the time it burnt itself out, over a thousand square miles

◁
After several decades, the young Sitka spruce and western hemlock standing on their nurse-log are well on their way to claim a place in the forest canopy

◁
Many years after its fall, a nurse-log has completely rotted away, but the trees it brought into existence are now mature and stand in a straight line supported by stilt-like roots. British Columbia

of bushland had been devastated. Two thousand homes were destroyed. Seventy-six people died.

The severity of the fire may well have been increased by the very success of fire precautions in previous years. That had allowed dead wood to build up on the floor of the forest so that when the fire eventually broke out, it burnt for much longer and more fiercely in any one place than it would have done otherwise. As a result even the biggest trees were engulfed in flames and lost their lives, just as so many other inhabitants, animal and human had done. But fire on a smaller scale is essential for the survival of this forest. Without great accumulations of dead vegetation on the ground, it travels fast, consuming the dry leaves and twigs, lingering a little longer in the fallen logs, licking up the trunks of the tree ferns and roaring through their arching crowns. The mountain ash aids the speed of the fire's progress, for it characteristically produces long strips of dry bark that become detached from the trunk and hang down like ribbons. They catch light and, blown by the wind generated by the flames, travel ahead of the main fire. But the mountain ash trunks are so straight and tall and in their lower parts so free of branches, that the flames are normally unable to reach the crowns of the biggest of them.

After only an hour or so, the main fire has passed. A few bigger logs on the ground continue to smoulder, puffs of smoke jetting out occasionally from their sides, and their interiors still glowing red. Where once there was a tangle of shady green leaves, there is now open space and for the first time in decades, sunlight strikes the ground. The air is pungent with the smell of burnt gum. The trunks of those trees that are still standing are scorched and the ground is black. Brush some of the soot away and you may find places where the soil has been baked a bright orange-red to a depth of several millimetres. You can see pale winding pathways that end in small holes in the ground. They were once the floor of tunnels through the undergrowth made by small creatures. They did not blacken because they had been kept clear of leaves by the scampering feet. Whether their creators have been roasted in their burrows or whether they were able to go down far enough for them to escape is too early to tell.

▷
A bush fire in southern Australia. Fuelled by the volatile gases given off by the blazing gum trees and fanned by the wind generated by its intense heat, such a great fire becomes unstoppable

And now, in a slow and gentle rain, the seeds of the mountain ash drift down to earth. They had hung in the branches for years, but the heat of the fire has cracked them open. A few seeds of understorey plants lying in the surface soil may have escaped damage by the flames, but any that were attached to the branches of smaller trees and bushes will have been destroyed along with those that bore them. So the mountain ash seeds have few competitors. Within a week or so they germinate. They sprout and grow so quickly that they stand around the pillar-like trunks of their parents as thick and as uniform as a crop of young wheat.

Ten years later, they are about six feet tall. They are still tightly packed, and grow so close to one another that their roots intertwine and form a dense mat. Few understorey plants are able to get a root-hold among them.

A further fifty years later and the passage of the fire is still marked by a dense stand of young mountain ash, all of a uniform age. But now the young mountain ash are beginning to compete among themselves. Differences between individuals are starting to appear. Some, either because they happen to grow on slightly more fertile ground, or because of their greater innate vigour, are rising above their companions, stealing their light. And beneath their developing crowns, tree ferns and other understorey plants are establishing themselves. The forest is slowly returning to its former state.

The threat to the survival of the spectacular forests of noble mountain ash is not, in fact, fire. It is the absence of fire. If the great trees die from old age before flames have cleared the ground for their seedlings, then they will leave no successors. Paradoxically, such a forest will not survive unless much of it is first destroyed.

◇

The plant communities that grow on the arid sandy lands of the south-western corner of Australia also depend upon fire for their survival but in a rather different way. The land here is so poor in nutrients and in summer so baked by the sun, that a forest of tall trees cannot grow. Instead there is a low bush mixed with a scatter of trees, few of which are more than twenty feet high. But what a bush it is! To visiting botanists, it is a wonderland with flowers of

△
Grass trees and eucalypts are typical of the western Australian bush

greatest beauty, few if any of which they can have seen growing in the wild before. For this one corner of the continent contains no less than twelve thousand different plant species and 87 per cent of them grow nowhere else in the world. This individuality stems from the fact that, fifty million years ago, Australia was partly covered by a shallow sea which separated the western part of the continent from the rest. As Australia gradually warmed, this sea dried up, but it left behind a wide expanse of sand, so that today the western corner is hemmed in by desert and its ancient isolation is still to some degree maintained.

Fire has regularly scoured this land throughout its recent geological history. The plants have evolved with it, so now they are not only well able to survive its ravages but have come to be positively dependent upon it and use it to their own advantage.

The eucalypts that grow here often take the peculiar form known as mallee. Species that elsewhere become normal-looking trees here grow in a such a different way that they might be thought to be a completely different kind. Instead of a single trunk that only branches some height above the ground, they have a massive root stock from which rise half a dozen thin trunks of uniform height.

To English eyes, it looks as though the tree has been coppiced. When fire sweeps through mallee, the slender trunks are often totally consumed and killed. But the root-stock, close to the ground or just below its surface, bears a ring of stout buds from which new stems rapidly sprout. They grow more quickly and vigorously than the old, partly because the ground has recently been fertilised by the ash of other plants in the community, and partly because, to begin with, there are few other survivors with such well-established root systems competing for those nutrients.

One member of the eucalypt family, the bottlebrush, produces spectacular clusters of scarlet flowers at the end of its stems. But it will not shed any seed they produce unless there is a fire. So examining a bottlebrush can reveal how long it is since fire passed that way. All you have to do is to count the number of clusters of seeds still attached along the branch and that will tell you how many years the plant has remained unburnt.

Banksias are spectacular evergreen bushes and trees related to the proteas of South Africa but, with the exception of one whose range extends into the Pacific, they are totally restricted to Australia. Of the 75 or so species that exist, 60 grow only in this south-western corner. Their strange inflorescences consist of several thousand small florets massed together in a single spike and arranged in vertical lines, that in some species have a gentle spiral twist. They may be yellow, grey, a handsome dark red or even be multi-coloured. They take several months to develop and then open over several weeks. Birds such as lorikeets and marsupials like the honey possum come to drink nectar from them and in the course of doing so pollinate them. Usually, however, only a small proportion of the florets produce seed. In some species, those that are unsuccessful remain attached to the flower head, forming a grey rather bristly fur.

It takes about a year for the seeds to mature. Like the bottlebrush, some banksias will not shed their seeds unless there is a fire. Indeed, it is almost impossible to remove them from the plant because they are held in hard woody two-valved capsules. But as the flames scorch the branches, the intense heat causes the capsules to open. Their front ends resemble pairs of brown lips on the side of the furry spike and together they give the whole fruit a strangely animated

▷
A honey possum collects nectar and, unintentionally, pollen, from the inflorescence of a giant banksia. West Australia

△
Banksia cones retain their seeds within tightly closed capsules (left) and may do so for many years. Only after a fire do the capsules open (right)

hobgoblin appearance that has led to banksia-men becoming characters in Australian children's stories. By releasing their seeds only in the wake of a fire, the banksias ensure that they fall on well-cleaned, brightly-lit ground recently fertilised with ash and so get the most favourable of starts in what is, even at best, an extremely harsh and demanding environment.

This country is also one of the headquarters of the grass tree. Although this strange plant does grow in other isolated pockets in the continent, it is nonetheless closely identified with the south-western corner. It is neither a grass nor is it a tree. It is a distant relative of the lilies. But it does have very long narrow leaves that resemble grass, and they are born in a great shock on the top of a stem that looks like the trunk of a tree and may be up to ten feet high. However the core of this trunk is not timber but fibre and what seems to be bark is, in fact, the tightly compacted bases of the leaves which are shed annually from beneath the crown as the plant grows higher. These bases are glued together by a copious flow of gum and they form a very efficient heat insulation. Since the plant sheds one ring of leaves annually, counting the rings of bases in this fire-proof jacket gives an indication of age and reveals that the grass trees not only grow only a foot or so in a decade but that a mature one may be about five hundred years old and therefore be the survivor of dozens of fires.

When the flames do come, they quickly burn off the great tuft of leaves which incinerate almost instantaneously in a shower of red sparks that fly high into the sky. But the stem, surrounded by its fire-guard remains unharmed and the leaves are quickly regrown. The fire, however, has an additional effect that initially is invisible. As all the vegetation goes up in flames, great quantities of ethylene gas are released. This permeates to the heart of the grass trees and causes a major change within them. A few months after the fire has passed and the leaves have regrown, a vertical green rod emerges from the centre of the leaves. It grows taller and taller until it may double the plant's height. Then, along its length emerge a multitude of tiny white flowers. It may be the production of ethylene on a vast scale following the fire that cues the flowering of almost all the adult grass trees in the bushland.

The fire also has a dramatic effect on smaller plants, even if they have not been burnt. Western Australia is famous for the beauty of

Fire travels swiftly through the western Australian bush. The long narrow leaves of the grass trees flame like torches but are soon consumed and the fire moves on, leaving the terminal buds of the grass trees undamaged
▽

◁

Four days after the fire has passed, the grass trees and the eucalypts are blackened stumps, but the capsules of the banksia cones have opened

▷

Seven weeks later, the leaves of the grass trees are a foot long but there is still no sign of life from the banksia trees or the eucalypts

◁

Thirteen weeks after the fire, the leaves of the grass trees are nearly two feet in length and the eucalypts are beginning to sprout

the small flowers that cover the ground at the beginning of the rainy season. They, like those that bring comparable colour to the arid lands of South Africa, are annuals. There are perennials, too, that after having disappeared from the surface of the ground in the dry season arise once more from bulbs and tubers. Many smaller bushes also contribute to the splendour of the spring displays. But rain is not the only necessary cue. Flowering is also greatly influenced by previous fires. Chemical substances in the smoke produced by the fire impregnate the surface layers of the soil. When, perhaps months later, rain does fall, it dissolves these chemicals and washes them down more deeply into the ground where they reach the dormant seeds. It is these substances that are the essential triggers for germination. Water by itself is not enough. Nor is this phenomenon limited to Australia. Seeds from African heathland plants have the same requirement. As a result of this discovery, botanical gardens all over the world are now able to germinate seeds that until recently had resisted all attempts to coax them into life. They are put into tents and smoke is puffed over them.

◇

Fire may be necessary for the continuation of many plant communities in Australia, but in Africa, it dictates the fundamental character of a great section of the continent and the very existence of vast numbers of its animals.

The typical landscape of eastern Africa is a rolling grassland thronged with vast herds of antelope and zebra, and patrolled by giraffe and elephants. Fires here, like those elsewhere in the world, may be started by lightning strikes, but they are also lit, regularly and deliberately, by human beings. There is good reason to think that people have been doing this for at least twenty thousand years, so long, in fact, that man-made blazes roaring across the plains must be regarded as just as natural and well established a phenomenon as the very existence of the herds of animals.

Grass on the African plains rarely grows above knee height. In the dry season, its leaves wither and catch light very easily. The flames move across the land very swiftly – so fast, indeed, that if you are in their path, you may have to break into a run to prevent yourself being overtaken. But, unless the country has been unburnt for some years so that there has been a build-up of trash, you face no real problem. The line of flames is only a few feet wide and it is quite easy to jump through them and emerge unscorched on the other side.

And there you can see on the blackened ground that, although the grass has lost all its leaves, the horizontal stems that lie close to the surface of the earth or just beneath it, are completely undamaged. And it is from the buds on these stems that new growth will come. When rain next falls, shoots will sprout within hours.

You may also find the young seedlings of acacia thorn bush. If they are only a foot high or less, their leaves and regenerative buds will have been in the hottest part of the flames and little will be left of them on the charred stem. Such seedlings cannot survive. As long as fires regularly burn here, the plains will remain the dominion of grass.

That suits the herds of game that graze the plains and depend upon grass for their food. One might suppose that the animals that crop leaves with such assiduity would be the enemies of the grass, but in the long term, they are its allies. Like the fire, they do not damage the horizontal stems. The grasses even have structures that make it easier for the animals to remove the leaves, for there are special points of weakness at the base of each blade. That gives a grazer an easier mouthful, but it also ensures that the all-important horizontal stem is not ripped out by its roots. That would certainly be the end of the grass plant. The acacia seedlings, however, are as easily destroyed by nibbling teeth as they are by fire. So as long as game feed here, the dominance of the grass seems assured.

How is it, then, that over many areas, there are wide patches of acacia scrub? How did they get their start? In good years, when the rains are abundant and the grass grows strongly, there will be a big increase in the numbers of game on the plain. As the dry season drags on however, so many mouths trim the grass with such severity that there is virtually nothing to fuel a fire. The animals themselves, having exhausted their food supply, begin to move away to look for better grazing elsewhere.

In the absence of both flames and biting teeth, the year's crop of young acacia seedlings have a chance. If they escape damage for four or five seasons, the probability of their survival soars. If they can gain a few feet in height before the next fire, their buds may be above the most damaging of the swiftly moving flames. Their small leaves, by now, are guarded by sharp thorns and they are of little temptation to habitual grass-feeders like antelope or zebra. Their branches start to spread, taking more and more of the light and eventually the grass cannot grow beneath them. So a tract of acacia bush appears on the plains, sometimes in a small patch, sometimes extending for many miles, with all its member trees of about the same size and age and standing on bare earth.

But the victory of such thorn bushes is not permanent. As they increase in size and produce more leaves, so they begin to attract the attention of those animals that habitually browse bush, such as

Elephants with their huge strength, vast appetites and powerful digestions can make a meal from most parts of acacia trees and totally destroy them in the process of doing so. Kenya
▽

giraffe and gerenuk. When they get bigger still, elephants start to rip off whole branches, chewing leaves, thorns, twigs, even the wood in the branch itself. Commiphora, a shrubby thorny tree belonging to the balsam family which produces a rubbery resin known as myrrh, also grows on these plains, if it gets the chance. Such trees are not to the elephants' taste. That, however, does not save them. The elephants deliberately push them over and then leave them uneaten. The groves of thorn trees are destroyed and light floods back on to the ground. Grass once more spreads over the site. So the whole cycle, that may have taken a man's lifetime to run its course, repeats itself.

You could claim that the elephants, by destroying the acacias and uprooting the commiphora, are in effect gardening, creating conditions in which one of their favoured food, grass, will continue to flourish and provide them with a good annual crop. But equally you could argue that the grass has recruited the elephants to help it extend its empire and by growing more leaves than it needs for its survival, and developing a structure which allows it to be cropped without lethal damage, it is simply paying its employees a decent wage that it can well afford.

If that were true, then the African grasses would not be the only members of their family to have benefited from such techniques. Ten thousand years ago, a small wild grass growing around the eastern end of the Mediterranean, developed seeds that, upon maturing, did not fall from the stem as others did, but remained attached to it. At that time, groups of unusually intelligent primates that habitually walked upright on their hind legs, were living in the area, hunting animals and feeding on roots and seeds. They had grasped the fact that plants grew from seeds and realised that those they valued for food could be encouraged to grow in convenient places and in concentrations that made gathering them less time-consuming. To do that, seeds had to be gathered and it was easier to collect those that remained fixed to the stem in dozens than to search the soil for those that had already fallen and pick them up one by one. So an alliance was formed between that particular kind of grass and humans. At the cost of losing a proportion of its seeds, the grass began to extend its range very significantly.

As human beings increased in number, so they needed more food and they cut down great areas of forest to turn them into fields where their favoured grass could grow. Today, the descendant of that early grass, wheat, has become one of the most successful plants the world has ever seen. With the help of plant-breeders it has increased its stature to many times its original size and it now reigns in vast uniform monocultures over huge areas of Europe, Australia and North America. The greatest and most extensive of forests have been felled to make way for it. Prairies that once supported a rich carpet of small plants have been ploughed and resown with it. Smaller plants that attempt to grow alongside it and compete with it for nutrients are poisoned and removed. With the help of humanity, wheat no longer faces a social struggle. It has eliminated it.

The prairies of North America, once covered by a rich variety of herbaceous plants and grazed by huge herds of buffalo, are now the exclusive domain of human beings and the wheat plant
▽

5

LIVING TOGETHER

THE CORALS that build reefs are animals. To call them plants is an elementary mistake that no naturalist ought to make. But it is an understandable one. After all, they do look like plants. Some are shaped like bushes with upward-growing twigs. There are rounded, dome-shaped ones like huge cushion plants. Others form great horizontal fans, reminiscent of the acacias that stand on the African plains. And all are dependent upon light, as plants are – they cannot grow where the waters are dark and murky, nor in depths so great that sunlight cannot reach them.

If you swim among these corals at night, their animal nature is immediately obvious. Vast numbers of organisms like tiny sea-anemones have emerged from their tiny cells and cover the surface of the branches like fur. These are the coral polyps and it is they that have secreted the huge limestone structures in which they all live. Each polyp is connected to its neighbours by threads that extend through tiny passages in the limestone, and each occupies a little

◁
The plant-like forms of stony coral, growing in the clear water of the Great Barrier Reef

▷
Tiny coral polyps carry brownish granules in their walls. These are plants, the microscopic algae on which the polyps depend

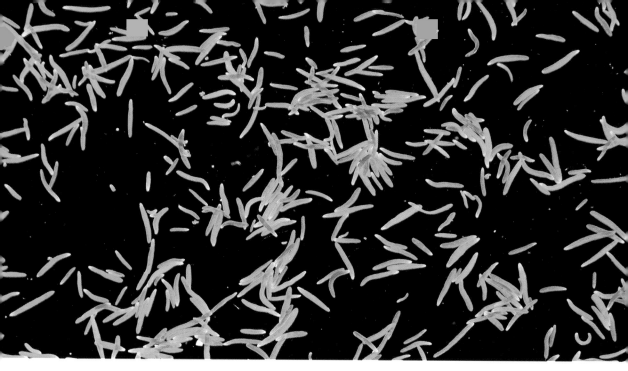

socket from which it protrudes in order to grope with its tentacles for edible particles in the water around it. They are, clearly, animals.

Why, then, do reef corals grow into such plant-like shapes? Because, although the polyps are not themselves plants, they have plants within them. The cells in the inner layers of the polyp's tissues contain tiny cells of an alga, complete with their grains of photosynthesising chlorophyll. And the polyp looks after its captives very well indeed, building its stony cup in a shape that ensures that they can get all the light they need.

Algae very similar to those in the corals float free in the open ocean. But very few can live in the seas around coral reefs for these waters, though rich in dissolved oxygen, are very poor in nutrients. Algae, like any other plants, need nitrates and phosphates, and that is exactly what the coral polyps, like any other animal, excrete in their waste-products. So those algae that are tucked away in the polyp's tissues, are provided with all the raw materials they need in order to flourish, yet are safe from the raids of hungry vegetarian grazers.

But the polyps extract a high rent from their lodgers. They secrete a digestive solution within their cells that weakens the skins of the algae and causes them to leak. Some 80% of all the food photosynthesised by the algae passes out of them and into the polyp's cells. The polyps are, as a consequence, so well-nourished that they have

△
These small marine worms owe their green colour to the algae which live in their tissues. At low tide, the worms lie on the surface of the sand to allow their algae to absorb the sunshine they need. As the tide comes in, the worms burrow down into the sand in order to maintain their position on the sea bed. Northern Europe

sufficient energy to spend on building their protective limestone skeletons. And the algae perform a further service. They manufacture a chemical that acts like a high-factor sun-cream shielding both themselves and their polyp hosts from the injurious ultra-violet rays, which in these tropical surface waters are very strong indeed.

Many other marine animals have gone into partnership with algae. The small archipelago of Palau in the western Pacific is formed by an ancient coral reef that once grew around the summit of an extinct volcano. Some twenty thousand years ago, changes in the ocean floor lifted the reef above the level of the sea. In some places, it collapsed onto itself, creating a number of basins which are now filled with sea water. Several have direct and easy access to the sea along wide channels, but one is connected only by the myriad tiny passageways which riddle the ancient coral. They are so narrow that no large creature can travel along them. But the water, surging through the coral, carries a multitude of microscopic larvae and among them are those of jellyfish. Once these have grown to any size, they cannot get back to the sea and today the lake, a mere two hundred yards or so across, is thronged with several billion jellyfish.

Such restricted waters might seem to be very poor in food of any kind, and were these jellyfish to live as most jellyfish do, by catching small fish and other animals with their stinging tentacles, then it could well be that they would not survive in such numbers. But these jellyfish live in a different way. They do not have stings. They are nourished instead by algae living within their tissues, in the same manner as their much smaller relatives, the coral polyps. This means, however, that unlike most other jellyfish, they must seek sunlight in order that the plants in their internal gardens remain healthy and productive. So every morning the immense fleet heads for the western side of the lake where the sun, rising above the steep walls surrounding the lake, first strikes its waters. As the sun moves across the sky, so the jellyfish travel towards it. The front of this great congregation forms a vertical pulsating wall that extends down in the water to a depth of a good twenty feet. In one or two places in the dark water beyond, a shaft of sunlight may shine through the trees and into the water and a few hundred jellyfish may hover within it, but otherwise, none of the millions ever enter the dark shadows. As the sun sinks below the western rim the

◁

The sunlight-seeking shoals of Jellyfish Lake in Palau, the western Pacific

jellyfish return towards the centre of the lake. With the coming of darkness, the jellyfish minister to the other needs of their internal plantations. Having given them sunshine, they provide them with mineral nutrients by descending into the still depths where the water is brown with decay and rich in nitrates.

This behaviour by such simple animals is certainly remarkable, but the mechanism which brings it about is not complex. The jellyfish have sense organs which are able to differentiate between greater and lesser intensities of light and the simple response of tilting their pulsing bells towards the brighter light is all that is needed to create the spectacular daily migrations.

The giant clam also keeps algae within its body. They are not imprisoned within its cells but held in a space directly beneath the outer skin of its mantle which is exposed to light whenever the two halves of the clam shell gape open. In some the mantle is purple, in others a vivid green, but always there are lines of bright spots along it. These are specially transparent patches that act like lenses, focusing light on the colonies of algae directly beneath. If the algae become too abundant, the clam thins them out by changing the constituents of its internal fluids and digesting some of them.

Colonies of algae grow in special compartments within the fleshy lips of giant clams. Malaysia

▽

Of all the reef creatures which cultivate algae within their tissues, sea-slugs are perhaps the most remarkable. They are molluscs that have lost their shells and therefore have little protection against fish. They live on coral and other similar organisms, munching their way through the polyps, each species with its own favoured kind of coral fodder. Many are difficult to see, for the colour of the tentacles that cover their backs match very closely the colour of the coral on which they graze. Indeed, in some cases it is literally identical. Much of the coral's colour comes from its internal algae. The sea-slug, when it eats coral, is able to separate these algae from the tissues of the polyp which it needs to digest. It then moves them from its stomach into its tentacles and keeps them there alive. As a result, the defence-less sea-slug acquires a near-perfect camouflage.

One sea-slug common on the Great Barrier Reef in Australia has taken this practice even further. It is able to stimulate its captive algae so that they proliferate to an unusual degree. To accommodate the greater numbers produced in this way, it develops branches in its gut which extend into leaf-like tentacles along its flanks. Having stocked its tentacles with plants, the sea-slug moves away from the

This sea-slug from the Great Barrier Reef keeps flourishing colonies of algae in the long tentacles that sprout from its back. It has so many colonies that it can live entirely on the food they produce
▽

feeding grounds among the coral where it first acquired the algae. It seldom if ever feeds on coral again. It is sustained entirely, it seems, by its internal gardens.

That an active animal should capture immobile plants and keep them for its own purposes inside its body, is not altogether extraordinary. After all, animals have always exploited plants. It is more surprising, perhaps, to discover that sometimes the arrangement is the other way round and that some animals live inside the bodies of plants – to the benefit of the plant.

The tenants are, very frequently, ants and they take up lodgings in a wide variety of plants. Some species of rattan are among them. Rattans, being a kind of palm, are nearly always unbranched and grow only from the bud at their tip. If that is destroyed, the whole stem, which may be immensely long, dies. The tip, however, is particularly good to eat. Animals such as squirrels, wild pigs and tapirs, if they can reach it, will tear away at the protective sheath in which it is swathed and consume the sweet young leaves. Accordingly, this end of the rattan is usually well protected by an armoury of exceedingly sharp spines. A few species have additional protection, as you will become sharply aware if you trip over one of their stems near the growing end or get caught in the spiny tendrils.

Suddenly there is a most alarming noise, something between a rustle and a hiss. It starts as a continuous sound and then develops into a pulsing throb. Your first reaction may well be that you have disturbed a snake or perhaps a wasps' nest – which might be even more unpleasant. A little cautious exploration soon reveals that the sound is coming from the rattan stem itself.

Those responsible quickly appear. Small black ants scurry out of a hole in one of the dry brown husks that encircle the main stem just above the point where each leaf stalk joins it. They repeatedly beat their heads on the husk in a threatening and angry way and soon begin to coordinate with one another to do so in unison. These sudden crescendos act as an alarm to those ants living in the next husk along the stem and soon the rattan for many yards of its length is rustling and hissing. It is a fair warning that if you persist in interfering with the rattan, you risk getting badly bitten.

The rattan does not reward the ants in any way for acting as its defendants, except by providing them with a home inside the dead leaf-bud husks. But it pays indirectly. The ants tend herds of small aphids which suck the rattan's sap by inserting their tiny mouth-parts into its stem. They then excrete from the ends of their abdomens drops of a liquid, rather flatteringly called honey-dew, which the ants drink. So the rattan manages to keep a battalion of ferocious bodyguards to protect its tip and pays them by providing pasture for their dairy herds.

The situation, however, is not a static one. The rattan grows rapidly, continually putting out more leaves as its stem lengthens and its tip advances. Each leaf bud has its own husk and the ants, obligingly, shift up the stem, moving into the new accommodation as soon as it becomes available, taking their larvae and their aphid herds with them. It may be that they have to do this because the aphids can only extract their drinks from the young tender tissues of the rattan. But the result is that the rattan's growing tip gets continuous protection.

It is easy to imagine how such a partnership might have started. Ants have a liking for small cavities in which to live. The protective leaf-husks of the rattan are an obviously suitable home. But the rattan actively encourages the ants to become tenants by growing husks that are specially dilated and thus make particularly spacious dwellings.

◇

Acacias, both in Africa and America, do a similar thing – and more. Their own defences against browsing animals are long, strong thorns. The bull's horn acacia of South America grows a particularly spectacular kind, a pair each a couple of inches long, joined together at the base and flaring outwards in just the way the name of bull's horn would suggest. But they are to be feared for something in addition to their sharpness. Soon after the acacia grows one, a queen ant who has already mated lands upon it and gnaws a hole near the tip, just big enough to allow her to crawl into the hollow base. There she lays her eggs.

The young workers, when they hatch, come out of their thorn home every day and patrol the stems and leaves of the surrounding shoots, hunting for insects that may land on the acacia in order to

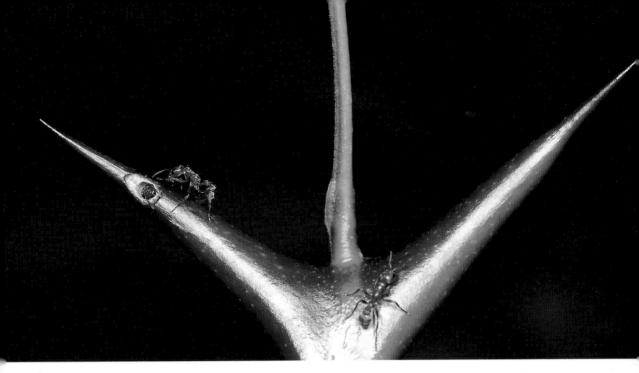

△
Ants emerge from their home within the thorn of an acacia. Costa Rica

The acacia provides its lodgers with nectar from special glands on its stems
▽

nibble its leaves. Any that do arrive are promptly eaten – which suits the acacia. As the queen continues to lay, the colony may grow so large that the workers spread from the original shoot on to others nearby and even take up lodgings in more thorns. Eventually the time comes when they encounter worker ants from another similar colony elsewhere in the tree. Then there is a battle. The rival armies engage with great ferocity. Limbs are severed. Contestants are thrown bodily from the branches. In the end, the colony with the biggest army almost certainly wins.

The ants are fighting for more than their homes within the thorns. They are also defending a very special supply of food and drink. The acacia produces nectar from glands placed not within the flowers, as they are when a plant needs to attract pollen-carrying insects, but along the lower part of the leaf-stalks. And the nectar flows not just during the flowering season but all the year round. The plant also provides solid food in the form of small orange beads, rich in fat, that develop on the tips of the leaflets. These are so well suited to the ants' diet that young larvae can take them neat. A worker cuts up the beads into pieces and stuffs a fragment into a special pocket on a larva's underside, just below its head. The larva can then take a bite whenever it wishes by bending down its head and sticking its jaws into the pocket.

What reward does the acacia get for such lavish hospitality? It is, certainly, kept free of insect pests that might damage its leaves or suck its juices. The ants fall upon them and eat them with vigour. That this is truly a valuable service has been demonstrated experimentally by removing the thorns and the ants within them. Undefended, the tree suffers badly and may not even survive. Since the ants eat the insects they kill, it might be thought that they would behave in the same way whether the acacia rewarded them or not. But they do other things that seem to serve only their landlord and to be of no direct benefit to themselves. They regularly travel down the trunk of the acacia and chew and destroy any seedlings of other kinds of plants that might germinate within a radius of about a foot, keeping the acacia free of competing plants on the ground. Nor will the ants allow other plants to approach from above. If the branch of a neighbouring tree touches the acacia, the ants cross over on to it and mutilate its leaves and buds so severely that the rival branch dies back.

One group of plants, the ant-plants, provide even more lavish accommodation for their ant-lodgers. They are epiphytes, and are very common growing on the branches of mangroves. In such a position, without roots in the ground, they are in particular need of mineral nutrients. Their guests provide it. The ant-plant's stem is swollen into a globe the size of a football and armoured on the outside by prickles. Ants swarm all over it, scurrying in and out of holes on the surface. Within, there are a number of large inter-

◁
Small fatty beads grow from the tips of the acacia's leaflets which the ants harvest. Costa Rica

△

Within, the plant is honeycombed by chambers which the ants use as living quarters, nurseries, royal apartments and middens. Indonesia

◁

The ant plant grows attached to the branches of mangroves (above). Its surface is pocked with tiny apertures, gateways through which ants run in order to reach their homes inside (below)

connected chambers. Some are the ants' living quarters. There the queen sits, steadily producing her eggs, and there too are the nurseries where the young larvae are kept and reared. These apartments have smooth light-coloured walls. But other chambers are different. These have darker walls which are covered with small warty outgrowths. Here the ants deposit the remains of their insect meals and their droppings. Both are rich in phosphates and nitrates, exactly the nutrients that the plant badly needs since, hanging on the branches of a mangrove tree in a brackish swamp, it is cut off from the soil. It absorbs them through the walls of these compartments and so is able to flourish in one of the most difficult and impoverished of habitats for a plant. But it can only do so because its insect lodgers pay rent by feeding it.

◇

Surprising though it may seem, plants also form partnerships with fungi. Fungi, after all, are normally seen as the enemies of plants, not only destroying their bodies when they are dead, but battening upon them while they are alive and hastening their end. The ap-

pearance of a bracket fungus, spreading its great plates horizontally from the trunk of an aged oak, is often regarded as a sign that the old tree will not live for much longer. In fact, the fungus could well be the tree's saviour and enable its host to live longer than it would do otherwise.

△
A bracket fungus sprouting from the side of an ancient tree may seem to signal its imminent death, but in fact may well prolong its life

The bulk of the trunk of a mature oak, like that of any tree, is dead. Its living region is a relatively narrow band just beneath the bark. The cells on the inside of the band steadily develop into rigid thick tissues, so increasing the trunk's girth. As it ages, this material eventually forms the solid timber pillar in the heart of the tree. This provides support for the branches which keep the leaves within the reach of sunlight. But the central pillar is dead tissue. Producing it took a great deal of the oak's resources over its long life. The oak, by itself, cannot recover that investment. Its only chance of doing so is with the help of fungi.

A single spore of a bracket fungus, as small as a particle of dust and carried on the wind, may enter a tree through a wound in its bark. It develops into a thread which moves from fibre to fibre through the layer of living sapwood beneath the bark and then into the timber beyond. Once there, it begins to proliferate. Some kinds feed only on the colourless cellulose of the cell walls. Others are also capable of digesting lignin, the hard brown substance that a tree deposits within the cells that make up its timber. Many will remain dormant for years until the tree in which they are living is weakened by age. Perhaps it is struck by lightning. Maybe it loses a branch in a gale. Then the fungal threads begin to multiply prodigiously. They spread so fast and feed so effectively that the centre of the old tree starts to disintegrate.

It is only at this stage that we are likely to be aware of the presence of the fungus, for now its fruiting body begins to sprout from the side of the tree. This is a huge brownish structure like one or more rounded shelves, sometimes two or even three feet across. At certain times of the year, pores fall from tiny holes on the underside of these shelves and do so in immense numbers. A big bracket fungus is estimated to produce twenty million spores every minute and it may continue to do so for five months. If the sun is shining from behind, the microscopic spores catch the light and look like smoke so that the bracket seems to be smouldering. Because this first visible sign of the fungus only appears when the tree is elderly or already stricken, it is usually assumed that it is the fungus that has infected the tree like a disease and is bringing about its death. But that is hardly just. The fungus has not attacked the living tissues of the tree, only the dead timber. And now, far from harming the tree, it brings it considerable advantages.

To start with, the remains of the wood, after the fungus has digested it, are in a form that the tree can absorb. So as this rotted pulp accumulates on the ground within the hollowed trunk, the oak puts out small roots into what was once its centre to reclaim some part of its lifetime savings. And there is new valuable nutriment there too. The hollow trunk has become an attractive home for animals. Bats roost in it, hanging from its walls. Owls nest there. And droppings from these creatures fall on to the ground within and provide further rich sustenance for the tree.

The removal of the tree's dead heart brings yet another advantage. The change of form from solid pillar to hollow cylinder alters the way in which the trunk reacts to mechanical stress. It is much more resilient and stable. The removal of many tons of timber also reduces the strain on the tree's elderly and doubtless somewhat decayed root system. The result is that an old hollow tree is often able to withstand a gale better than a younger undecayed one. In the ancient hunting parks of England such as Windsor, where trees stand out in the open, unprotected by others from the wind, it is by no means rare after a storm to discover that hollow oaks, four or five hundred years old, remain upright when younger ones, a quarter their age, have been blown over. Tree and fungus, each pursuing its own best interests, have come together to the benefit of both. It is a most fortunate conjunction. It probably started relatively recently in the history of both species, but it now happens so frequently that it could almost – if not quite – be called a real and regular partnership.

◇

The most intimate relationship between plant and fungus developed very, very much earlier. The first single-celled plants floated in the sea, as many kinds of algae do today. About four hundred million years ago, some managed to spread to the moist earth around the margins of fresh-water lakes and survived as a thin green dusting on the soil. There they encountered thread-like fungi which were also, around that time, beginning to colonise the land.

Where plants lived, plants died and the fungi were there to consume the remains. Doubtless at that early period they were living within the soil. Lacking chlorophyll, they could not manufacture complex organic substances for themselves. But, then as now, they were able to obtain some nutriment by secreting an acid and dissolving the minerals in rocks and the soil. So each organism had valuable commodities needed by the other. The fungi could absorb starches and sugars from the plants. The plants could extract minerals dissolved in the water that they took from the fungi. A partnership was established and the fungi enclosed the algae within their tissues in a most intimate embrace.

The partnership survives to this day in twenty thousand different forms. It is so close that each pairing looks like a single entity and naturalists give each of them a single name as though that were indeed the case. They are lichens. It was not until the last century that scientists, peering at them through microscopes, recognised that two very different organisms were involved.

▷
Some lichens grow as blisters like these, slowly extracting sustenance from rock in the Antarctic. Others, such as these in France (below), grow taller and develop into miniature bushes and thickets an inch or so high

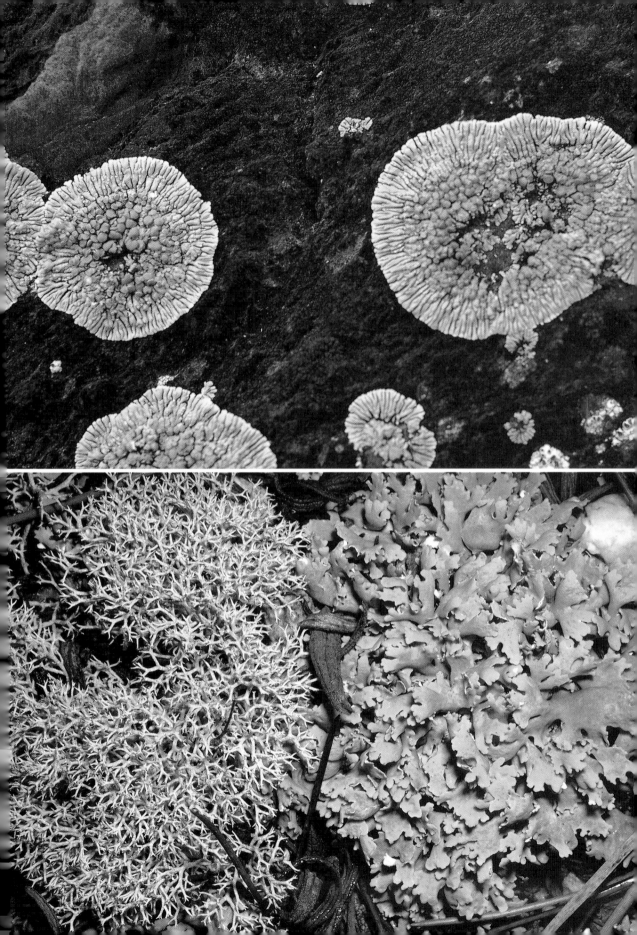

△
*The long grey
tufts hanging from
these trees in
Argentina are
formed by a lichen*

Some form thin skins on rocks and are often brilliantly coloured
– red, blue, yellow, green, even black. Others develop minuscule
branches and grow into dense curling thickets a few inches high.
Their outer skin is formed by the compacted threads of the fungi
and is sufficiently impermeable to prevent the loss of water from
the partnership; beneath are the algal cells, kept moist and protected
from harmful ultra-violet radiation by the fungal skin; and below
them, in the centre of the structure, there is looser tissue, also provided by the fungus, where food and water is stored.

The partnership has been extremely successful. Lichens can survive in the most extreme and severe of environments where neither
plants nor fungi can exist alone. In the Himalayan mountains, they
grow at altitudes of up to 18,000 feet. On the Antarctic ice-cap, they
have been found on rocks within 300 miles of the South Pole, where
it is so cold that growth is only possible for a few days in the year.

At the other end of the earth, in the Arctic tundra, lichens grow
with particular luxuriance. A bushy kind forms ankle-deep carpets
that covers great areas and grows in such quantities that it provides
the main food for reindeer in winter. This is the so-called reindeer

Lichens are one of the very few living organisms that can survive permanently on the continent of Antarctica

"moss". The long beards – bluish-green, grey or even yellow – that hang from the branches of trees in many northern forests are also, in fact, lichens. They obtain their moisture from mists and find all the minerals they need dissolved in the rain.

Lichens can also tolerate heat which would desiccate and kill most plants. They shrivel but remain alive and, when the opportunity comes, they take up moisture at extraordinary speed and in great quantities, absorbing as much as half their dried body weight in a mere ten minutes.

The fungal member of the lichen partnership reproduces by spores that develop inside special small cups and spikes. A single spore among the many millions blown from these structures is capable of founding a new colony but to do so it has to find a new algal partner. Exactly how it does this is even now not known. But the complexities of coordinating two separate sexual cycles appears to have defeated many lichens. Instead they produce small knobs containing representatives from both partners. These are blown away or transported inadvertently by insects. Travelling as a pair, they are ready to continue the alliance as soon as they arrive on a

suitable new site.

The algal partner is able to exist by itself and what is more will grow more swiftly when it does so. The fungus, however, cannot. To that extent, the fungus can be regarded as the ruler, clinging to life by holding the alga captive. In really harsh circumstances, the fungus will even kill and digest some of the algal cells, so confirming its dominance. In partnership, the two play an invaluable role in the living world. They are the intrepid pioneers. They establish themselves in some of the most hostile environments on the planet where nothing else can find food and when at last they die, the dust to which they are reduced may provide just enough nourishment to enable an independent plant to establish itself.

△
Lichens reproduce with small fruiting bodies. These red nodules each contain representatives of the lichen's two partners, the fungus and the alga

The lichen partnership is the closest and most intimate between plant and fungus but it is not the only one. Some of the early algae that first made the move from the sea to the land evolved into more complex structures and became green skins and furry mats. These were the ancestors of today's liverworts and mosses. Although they were green with chlorophyll and could therefore photosynthesise, they were only able to absorb the mineral nutrients they needed for the process if their surface was wet. They had no roots, only small wiry filaments that gave them a feeble attachment to the ground.

It was advantageous for them to grow tall, for then they were able to steal the light from their neighbours, but to do so they required a rigid stem. That in turn demanded better, firmer anchorage in the ground. Eventually they developed substantial outgrowths from the base of their stems that probed into the earth. These were the first true roots and they must have soon encountered the thread-like fungi in the soil. Once again, a physical connection between the two was established and once again there were such important benefits for each party that the relationship has survived until today.

Over three-quarters of all living plants still have underground fungal partners. The cables, ropes and strings, some running deep into the ground, that most of us think of as being the main roots of a tree, serve primarily as anchorage. The crucial business of collecting water and nutrients is done by a tangle of small hairy rootlets only a few inches down in the soil. That, after all, is the best place to collect liquids seeping down from the surface. It is here that the threads of the fungal partners also grow. They are physically attached to the tree's rootlets, penetrating their surface, some superficially, some deeply. They may invest the whole length of a root hair as a sheath or just be concentrated around its tip, and they extend into the soil to form a fine mesh that stretches far beyond the reach of the tree's rootlets and often connects with the fungal threads growing on the roots of neighbouring trees so that the whole forest floor is underlain by a continuous fungal mat. That this is so has been demonstrated by injecting substances with radioactive markers into one tree and then detecting their eventual appearance in the others growing nearby.

These partnerships are known as mycorrhizae, a name which means simply and accurately 'fungus-root'. Many thousands of different species of fungi take part in them. Although they depend upon their plant partners for much of their food, they live otherwise independent lives. In due season they reproduce. Some erect their fruit-bearing bodies above ground as mushrooms, toadstools and puffballs. Some trees may have several different kinds of fungal partners, but others link themselves with only one. Mycorrhizal fungi are also variable in their partnering. But some do form regular associations so fungus hunters know that a particular kind of toadstool is only to be found beneath the boughs of a certain kind of tree, such as a birch or a larch.

Some mycorrhizal fungi do not even emerge above ground to distribute their spores. They develop their fruiting bodies within the earth. These are the truffles and the false truffles. To recruit the messengers needed to distribute their spores, they use a perfume that seeps up through the soil. Human gourmets who relish the taste of truffles are seldom if ever able to detect the smell, but sows, which also like truffles, are able to do so with ease. This is hardly surprising because the scent produced by the truffle is chemically identical with that produced as a sexual signal by a boar. So properly harnessed, sows can show their human masters where these delicacies lie. These days, dogs are more widely used. They have the most sensitive of noses and they are easily trained – and doubtless they are more easily controlled than a sexually expectant sow.

Other animals are also coaxed by these reticent underground fungi into becoming their spore distributors. Beetle larvae burrow down to them, gorge on their substance and then pupate within them so that the adults, when they emerge, carry the spores away. Deer, mice and shrews in Europe, armadillos and opossums in South America, wallabies in Australia, all have a taste for particular truffles. The spores pass through their guts and are left with their droppings.

In the great coniferous forests of the American Pacific coast, flying squirrels regularly plunder these underground treasures. The duet of interdependence now becomes a trio. The squirrel gets food from the fungus and lodging from the tree, for it habitually nests inside holes in the trunks; the conifer gets nutrients from the fungus; and the fungus gets starches and sugars from the tree, and transport for its spores from the squirrel.

△
Indian pipe, a relative of the heathers and rhododendrons, rising from the ground in the coniferous forests of North America

This harmonious trio, here and there, may even become a quartet. But the new member introduces a dissonant note. Its ghostly pale stems rise up through the leaf litter in the darkest, gloomiest parts of the forest to a height of about ten inches. Each carries, at the tip, a white waxy flower. So lacking is it in pigment that it is sometimes called the corpse flower, but it is more generally known as the Indian pipe. Its leaves are no more than small colourless scales pressed close to the stem. Lacking chlorophyll, they are quite incapable of manufacturing food. The plant nourishes itself in a different way. Its roots reach down and fasten on to the fungal mat and from that absorbs all its nutriment. This food, of course, has not been produced by the fungus. It has come from the tree. But the Indian pipe, unlike the fungus, appears to give nothing whatever in return to either the fungus or the tree. It must be rated a parasite.

The contribution made by mycorrhizal fungi to their plant partners is not limited to nutrients. They are often essential for the plant's reproduction. The North American pine forests are dark places, for the thick foliage of the tall trees screens the sun from the

forest floor. A young seedling cannot get enough light to photosynthesise for itself and will not grow properly in sterile soil. But if the
seed falls on to ground where there is a thick mycorrhizal mat, then
the developing roots link with the fungal threads and through them
the infant tree gets the food it needs – food which comes, by way
of the fungus, from its parent or neighbour. At this stage, it is just
as much a parasite as the Indian pipe. No pine seedling will survive
in these shady forests unless it germinates in the fungal nurseries
and the mycorrhizal connection a young plant establishes at this
time will remain with it all its life.

Fungal nursemaids are employed by many plants, but for none
are they more important than orchids. Most plants provide their
seeds with food stores of some kind. But not orchids. Their seeds
are so small they verge on the invisible and getting them to germinate, as orchid fanciers the world over know only too well, can be
extraordinarily difficult. Some spectacular specimens have fetched
fantastically high prices precisely because they belong to species
that are very rare in the wild and have never produced germinating
seed in cultivation. The reason for their failure is that in the wild
they habitually establish a partnership with a particular species of
mycorrhizal fungus. No other kind will do. In cultivation, away
from their native forests and in glass-house conditions, these mycorrhizae do not exist or struggle to survive. The problem was
solved in the 1930's by germinating the seeds on a specially enriched
jelly which supplies the seedlings with the nutrients that in their
original homes their mycorrhizal fungi would have provided for
them. In recent years, ways have been discovered of identifying and
culturing their fungal partners so that now, theoretically, it is possible to germinate the seeds of all species of orchids.

Once the orchid has a proper start in life, the fungal connection
may be abandoned. But some species retain it permanently and, like
the Indian pipe, draw all their sustenance from their fungus partner which, in turn, extracts it from a tree. One of these is the bird's
nest orchid. It is found in beechwoods in many parts of Europe,
and gets its name from the curious mass of stumpy roots that
grow in all directions around its short thick central stem. These
link it with a fungus that feeds on the rotting leaves on the forest
floor. From the centre of this untidy bundle in June springs a stem

△
The bird's nest orchid takes nine years to reach maturity and produce its flowers. Having set seed, most then die. Southern England

eighteen inches or so tall which carries a spike of yellowish-brown flowers.

Another European orchid, the ghost orchid, is even more reduced. It lacks not only leaves, but true roots and exists only as a multi-lobed underground stem which carries a few sparse hairs connecting it to its mycorrhizal fungi. Without proper roots it is difficult for it to collect liquid and it lives only in woods that are so dense that sunlight seldom if ever reaches the ground and there is no risk of the soil drying out. In Britain it is considered to be the rarest of all native plants for it has been found only in two or three localities and even there it disappears for such long periods that several times it has been thought to have become extinct. This is because it will live for many years without flowering and remains hidden out of sight below ground feeding on its mycorrhizal fungi, slowly adding more lobes to its stem. If the spring is particularly wet, however, the plant may be stimulated to send up a pinkish stem through the moist soil to stand six or seven

The ghost orchid spends so much of its time underground, flowers so irregularly and grows in so few places, that it has several times been declared extinct in Britain – only to reappear

This orchid from western Australia has a totally subterranean life. It even blooms below ground. It has only been found in Western Australia and even there only on very few occasions and by accident

inches high above the carpet of dead leaves. In the summer this produces five to seven flowers with yellow petals and a large pink lip. Bumble bees will visit it to gather its nectar and so be laden with its pollinia, but the plant only rarely sets seed. It reproduces itself instead with buds that develop on thread-like underground stems growing out from the main lobes.

The most extremely adapted of all these parasitic orchids grows in western Australia. It blooms underground and never emerges above the soil at all. Not surprisingly it has only been seen on very few occasions – and then largely by accident. At the start of the autumn rains, the orchid produces a tulip-shaped structure which grows upwards, lifting the surface of the earth immediately above so that cracks form, from which drifts a faint perfume. This attracts a variety of insects, including fungus gnats and termites which crawl down to the buried flowers. It is the first plant known to recruit the help of termites as pollinators. It might seem surprising that these most abundant and widespread of tropical insects are not more widely employed but termites are just as shy of light as any fungus, so the only flower that could attract them is one which has the bizarre habit of blooming below ground.

◇

In the same way as some plants develop close relationships with animals, and others with fungi, so there are some that do so with other plants. The Christmas tree is one of the most glorious plants in all the west Australian heathlands. It is also one of the tallest, growing to 45 feet high. During December and January, when the summer is at its hottest and most of the flowers for which this part of the country is famous have died, the Christmas tree comes into blossom, its leafy branches thickly loaded with glorious orange-gold flowers. It seems to have a source of water that the withered plants around it lack. That is not exactly the case. The fact is that the Christmas tree steals the water that its neighbours have managed to extract from the parched ground before they themselves are able to make use of it. When one of its roots meets that of another plant, it develops a small white sucker which clamps on to the root of the neighbour and grows into a little white collar completely encircling it. A pair of sharp woody pincers then develops from the side of the collar opposite the point where the sucker first made contact with the root. This unique structure grows inwards and completely severs the water-carrying tubes in the root. At the same time the sucker develops vessels which grow into the root's wound, connect with both sides of the cut and divert the liquid carried by the root back to the Christmas tree.

With this technique repeated many thousand times in the ground all around it, the Christmas tree steals water and mineral nutrients

▷

The Christmas tree of western Australia is one of the very few plants that flower at Christmas, in the middle of the southern summer

from plants growing over a huge area of bush. Its roots, in their search for victims, may extend for as much as a hundred yards from its trunk. It will parasitise several different plant species at the same time. Banksias, paperbark trees, acacias, grasses, even introduced plants like roses and carrots are all attacked. Indeed, it is surprisingly indiscriminate.

Some years ago, scientists working for the space programme decided to build a receiving station in western Australia. The various installations in the bush were connected by underground cables. But soon after the system was completed, faults began to develop and communications with distant stations were repeatedly broken. It was some time before the Christmas tree was identified as the culprit. Its roots were attacking the cables, cutting right through the plastic covering and down to the copper core. The problem became widely recognised and telecommunications companies, working in western Australia have accepted that in a year every hundred miles of cable is likely to be attacked forty or fifty times. When fibre-optic cable was introduced, this proved equally attractive to the Christmas tree roots. It now seems that the only solution, albeit an expensive one, is to make cable so thick that it is beyond the grasp of the Christmas tree's parasitising collar.

The Christmas tree is a member of the mistletoe family, one of the very few that grows into a free-standing tree. It is, nonetheless like all its relations, a parasite, for although a seedling can survive independently for about a year, it must thereafter fasten on to another plant if it is to survive. The family itself is huge, with over a thousand different species, most of which live in the tropics. Like the Christmas tree, they have green leaves and can therefore manufacture food for themselves, but they are wholly reliant on their hosts for liquids. The vast majority, however, do not parasitise other plants through the roots. Instead they fasten themselves directly on to the trunk or a branch of a tree.

A dwarf member of the family parasitises the ponderosa pines in the south-west of the United States. It encloses each of its tiny 3-millimetre long seeds in a small berry. As the berry ripens, the pressure within it builds up. Its connection with its stalk becomes increasingly weakened until suddenly it breaks, explosively. The skin of the berry contracts and the tiny seed, blunt at the front end

△

The pine mistletoe,
a dwarf member of
the family,
parasitises several
species of conifer in
North America

and pointed at the back, an excellent aerodynamic shape, shoots out at an extraordinary speed. The action is very like that of the squirting cucumber, but the seed's velocity is even greater. It has been calculated to be moving at a rate of 45 feet a second as it leaves its launcher and it is capable of travelling nearly fifty feet. The seed's coating is so sticky that it adheres to whatever it lands on.

In spite of the fact that this explosion is one of the most violent in all the plant world, it is unlikely to carry the seed very far beyond the host tree. Most mistletoes rely instead on birds to take their seeds to new victims.

The only European mistletoe is the strange twin-leaved parasite that once played an important part in humanity's fertility rites, perhaps because in winter its leaves remain green and visibly alive when those of the tree on which it grows have all fallen. It still provides a licence for men and women who may be strangers to kiss beneath it at Christmas time. Its white berries have flesh that is so extraordinarily sticky that when a bird such as a thrush or a blackbird tries to eat them, they often become stuck to its beak. The bird finds this so irritating that it tries to wipe the berry off by scraping it on to another branch and in doing so, rams it into a crevice. The seed then puts out a root which worms its way into the tree and eventually connects with the vessels within the branch that carry the tree's sap. And with that as food, it flourishes.

Australia is particularly rich in mistletoe species, with some seventy-five of them living in all kinds of country from mangrove swamps to high mountain forest. Some grow on a variety of tree hosts. Others restrict themselves to just one. Many have leaves that, most remarkably, closely resemble those of their host. It is difficult to account for this by the usual evolutionary argument that the resemblance brings the mistletoe some advantage such as camouflage. It is more likely that when it takes water and nutriments from its host, it also absorbs some of the growth hormones that influence leaf shape with the result that host and parasite come to resemble one another.

As a group, the Australian mistletoes have developed a rather more specialised system of transport than that employed by their European relative. One particular bird, the mistletoe bird, eats little

◁
An Australian mistletoe growing on a eucalypt

An Australian male mistletoe bird collects a sticky berry

other than mistletoe berries. There are so many species, each with its own fruiting season, that the bird is able to find berries throughout the year and it flies along regular migration routes in order to do so.

Its digestive system is specially modified to cope with this diet. For some reason, it processes the berries with remarkable speed so that one will take less than half an hour to travel from entry to exit. When it emerges, the seed still has considerable residual stickiness and so remains fastened to the bird's rear. The defecating bird does not, however, sit transversely across a twig waiting for the mistletoe seed to drop off. Instead, it turns so that its body is aligned along the twig and carefully wipes its bottom on the bark beneath. This fixes the seed to the tree but threads of the seed's glue still remain attached to the bird's rear and it has to make three separate sideways jumps along the twig before the connection is finally broken.

One does wonder why the bird persists with such an infuriating diet.

Some plant parasites have even lost their leaves. They are thus totally dependent upon their hosts not only for water but for most of their sustenance. Dodder is one of them. It is related to convolvulus and like that common, aggressive and tenacious plant, it travels into new territory by winding tendrils around the stems of other plants. The convolvulus has well-developed roots and underground stems – only too well-developed for those gardeners who are trying to eradicate it from their flower beds – and it climbs only to get a place in the sun for its leaves and its handsome white flowers. Dodder, however, is more sinister. It not only actively hunts, probing through the undergrowth with its tendrils, but selects its victims with care. It seems able to tell whether a particular stem it touches is rich in nutriment or not. If it encounters one that is thin and impoverished, its tendril will leave it and continue to explore, seeking a better plumper victim. When it does so, the tendril wraps around the stem and then attaches itself to it with a swollen sucker. Small threads developing from it then invade the stem. Within hours the tendril has expanded visibly. With its new source of energy, it may either flower or produce another tendril that carries on the search.

△
The mistletoe's berry, even after it has passed through a stomach, is still so sticky that the mistletoe bird has considerable difficulty in detaching it

▷
Dodder, an aggressive parasite, sprawls over heather. Britain

Nor is this strange rudimentary species the most extremely reduced of plant parasites. On top of a tiny pillar of rock standing in the sea just off the Maltese island of Gozo grows one of the rarest of all Mediterranean plants. It is called locally the Maltese fungus. In fact it is not a fungus but a true flowering plant. Most of its life is spent underground, drawing its nourishment from the roots of tamarisk or sea lavender. At this stage it consists of no more than a stem from which sprout the many suckers that attach it to the roots of its host. Its leaves have been reduced to just a few tiny scales on the stem's surface. But in the summer it sends up a number of thick spikes which break through the ground and stand several inches high. They are covered with a multitude of tiny red flowers, packed so tightly together that they look like a rather coarse fur. Some of them are male, some are female, and some contain both an ovary and stamens. As the weeks pass, they are fertilised by flies. The flowers then wither and the spike turns black.

The rarity and mysterious character of this plant led the Maltese in mediaeval times to attribute strange powers to it. The apothecaries believed in sympathetic magic. One of its basic principles was that a cure will carry a physical hint of the disease for which it is appropriate. They therefore decided that since the flowers were red and turned black as they dried, the plant would be certain to help with problems connected with the blood. So it was used to staunch wounds. Not only that, but its phallic shape also suggested that it would be helpful in the treatment of sexual problems. Such twin talents coupled with its extreme rarity made the plant very valuable indeed.

When the Crusaders occupied the Maltese islands in the sixteenth century, they fully appreciated what a treasure they possessed. Permanent guards were stationed on the coast opposite the rock to protect it against thieves. The sides of the islet were trimmed of any projecting ledges that might provide footholds for anyone trying to climb it. A thief who was caught attempting to steal the plant would be punished by being sent in chains to row in the galleys. The dried spikes were not only used by the Crusader Knights after their battles but were sent by their leader, the Grand Master of the Knights of St John of Jerusalem, as special presents to the crowned heads of Europe. They were gifts that no-one else could make.

▷
The mysterious flowers of the misnamed Maltese fungus rise from the ground on the shores of the Mediterranean Sea

△
The flower bud of rafflesia emerges from the floor of the rain forest in Borneo

The most dramatic of all plant parasites, however, exists not hidden underground but actually within the tissues of another plant. It lives in Borneo and Sumatra. Its host, a vine, hangs down from the rain forest trees. In places where it trails along the ground, but at largely unpredictable times, a lump develops on the vine's bark. Week by week this grows bigger and bigger until it erupts and sits, like a large cabbage wrapped in its tightly closed leaves, in a small woody cup that has been developed by the vine. Then one night, the leaves unfold and reveal themselves to be enormous leathery petals. There are five of them. Their surface is orange, mottled by cream-coloured patches that are raised like weals. They surround a deep central chalice on the floor of which stands a round disc on a pedestal. The disc is covered by a multitude of large vertical spikes, and beneath its rim, on the pedestal, there are the sex organs. Some flowers are male, some female. The whole flower is frequently as much as 36 inches across. The record is said to be 42 inches. The titan arum which grows in many of the same forests is certainly larger, but it contains within its spathe a multitude of small flowers and it therefore has to be classed as an inflorescence. This bloom, lying flat on the forest floor, is a single flower – and the largest in the world.

△
Over several days it swells to the size of a cabbage and unfolds its leathery petals

The first European to publish a description of it was Thomas Stamford Raffles, the founder of Singapore and, at the time of his discovery, the Governor of a short-lived British colony in Sumatra. It was named, in his honour, rafflesia. Since his time more than a dozen other species related to this giant, have been found elsewhere in south-east Asia, but they are all somewhat smaller.

The vine that rafflesia parasitises is abundant in the forests and easy to find. Were it less so, it might make the search for rafflesia itself somewhat easier. As it is, there is no way of telling which of the many vines you identify as being the right kind will be harbouring the parasite. The first sign you are likely to discover is a row of perhaps half a dozen buds, of increasing size bulging from the ground where a slumped length of the vine is thinly covered by soil. But even then, you cannot be certain of seeing the flower, for the buds take many weeks to grow to full size and even when they have done so, they seem to hover on the brink of opening for many days. During all this time they are susceptible to damage by forest animals. A significant proportion of them – some say as much as two-thirds – unaccountably rot even before they open.

Fully open, the rafflesia flower may be as much as three feet across
▷ ▷

It is often claimed that the flower, when at last it does open, has the repulsive smell of rotting flesh and that the local people therefore call it the "corpse flower". The Indonesian name, bunga patma,

△
A fly visiting rafflesia is given a dab of pollen on its back

does not however refer to either corpses or death. It means, rather more appealingly, "lotus flower", for the lotus is a symbol of fertility and the swelling bud of rafflesia could hardly be a more powerful image of pregnancy. Certainly, the ones we found had no dreadful stench. On the contrary, they had a cool, moist, delicate perfume rather like fresh mushrooms.

◁
In the depths of the chalice of rafflesia's flower stands a spiked disc on a pedestal. The stamens grow from beneath its rim

The great flower is pollinated by small flies. They alight on the disc, crawl over its rim and on to its underside which is thickly covered with dark red hairs. These may serve in some way to guide the flies towards the sex organs. While we watched them arriving, a small spider also appeared and started to construct its web between the petals and the central disc, capitalising on the flower's ability to provide fly bait.

After three days, the scent seemed to become more acrid and unpleasant, with the tang of rotten fish to it, though whether this

△
*A little tree-shrew
visits the huge
flower. It may be
responsible for
spreading
rafflesia's seeds*

came from its perfume or its petals which were blackening and starting to decay we could not tell. After four days, the whole structure had collapsed into a black slimy mass.

Female flowers are much rarer than males and seem to have little success in getting pollinated, for rafflesia fruit is only rarely discovered. It is a sphere, six inches across, with a woody, brownish surface and filled with a smooth, oily cream-coloured flesh in which there are thousands of red-brown seeds. Tree-shrews and squirrels come to eat at it, scooping out the flesh with their paws. Doubtless, they then distribute the seed, either in their fur and on their paws, or in their droppings. Whether on germinating, the seeds are capable of making their own way into a vine stem, or whether they have to be provided with an entry point by their carriers gnawing the vine bark, is not known.

Why should the flower be so extraordinarily big and out of all proportion to the rest of its body, the threads hidden within the tissues of the vine? Its wide-spreading petals cannot assist in the dispersal of its scent, as the tall spadix of the titan arum almost certainly does. The usual explanation of the development of extravagantly large flowers is that they are the result of competition between rival plants for the services of pollinators. But that hardly seems likely to anyone who has spent any time in the humid gloom of the Bornean rain forest persecuted by flying insects of one kind or another. There seems to be no shortage of them.

Plants, like any other living thing, are ruled by cost-efficiency budgets. The food and energy they expend in growing flowers, leaves or any other organ must normally bring a commensurate advantage of some kind. But rafflesia may not be so curbed. It does not, after all, earn the food it expends. It takes it straight from the vine. Provided the vine is not weakened by the loss to the point of death, there seems to be no limit to the amount rafflesia may extract and therefore no limit to the size of flower it constructs. Maybe an unearned income in the plant world, as elsewhere, can lead to profligacy and extravagance on a truly monumental scale.

6

SURVIVING

ONLY FOUR things are essential for plants – water, light, warmth, and a modicum of minerals. The list is very modest. It seems particularly so when one discovers how little of any of these things some plants require. Any place that can provide a mere trace of each, for even a limited period of the year, will be colonised by plants of some kind. But without something of all four, no plant can live for long.

One place denies them that – the South Pole. There, in recent years, human beings have established an outpost for themselves. To do so they had to build a huge metal dome under which they created an artificial environment to give them the warmth, the light and the food stores that they require. But outside its shelter, on the bare ice, no living thing can survive for any length of time.

The vast Antarctic ice-cap holds three-quarters of all the world's fresh water. At the Pole, it is three miles thick. Since plants require fresh water, they might seem, on that score at least, to be well provided for here. But plants can only make use of water in its liquid form. As a solid it is not available to them. What about light? The sun, even in summer never rises high in the sky and in the autumn begins to sink lower and lower until eventually it disappears alto- gether and leaves the South Pole in darkness for almost half the year. Warmth? The coldest temperatures ever recorded on earth, minus 88 degrees Centigrade, were recorded on the ice cap at Vos- tok, the Russian Antarctic station. Whatever heat a living creature might generate in its body is sucked out by winds that scream across the ice at 120 miles an hour. The Pole has no liquid water, no warmth and for half the year, no light. So it has no life.

Yet within three hundred miles of this unrelentingly hostile place, there are plants, algae, living in partnership with their ancient allies,

△
*Lichens grow
particularly well on
rocks that are used
as a regular perch
by birds such as
this Antarctic tern,
for the birds' drop-
pings provide an
exceptionally rich
source of nutrients*

fungi, as lichens. They blister the rocky tips of the mountains that, in some places project through the blanket of ice. But these hardiest of colonists can only just manage to survive. There may be no more than two or three days in a year when the temperature rises sufficiently for them to activate their body chemistry. Then, for just a few hours, the fungus manages to dissolve an infinitesimal amount from the surface of the rock and extract a few minerals, and the algae to photosynthesise. So the lichen grows minimally before the whole partnership relapses again into frozen dormancy.

Some of these Antarctic lichens are black and use what little heat they can absorb from the feeble rays of the sun to melt the snow around them as the skies lighten in spring. In the middle of the summer, however, their colour causes them to absorb enough heat to dry them out and they go into a state of suspended animation until the following winter. Growing alongside them are pale lichens. They have adopted exactly the opposite tactic. Their colour reflects much of the heat so they do not dry out and are able to photosynthesise throughout the warmest part of summer. But in the winter they get so cold that they too have to cease all activities.

The growth of these lichens is extraordinarily slow. They may take fifty or sixty years to cover a square centimetre, and the scarlet, yellow or greenish blotches that are several inches across may be hundreds, even thousands of years old. But you will only find those on larger rocks. A lichen that attempts to establish itself on a small boulder is likely to be exterminated before it has even properly started, for the ferocious wind is so powerful that it can overturn small rocks, leaving a young lichen on the underside and in total darkness. Not even a lichen can survive that.

A little farther away from the Pole, other algae succeed in establishing themselves without fungal help. At one place near the coast of the continent, a rank of high mountains holds back the ice which almost everywhere else, sweeps down into the sea. Here, in the Dry Valleys, there is more exposed rock than in all the rest of Antarctica put together. Outcrops of sandstone form high cliffs. Crack open a slab from one of the more sheltered parts and a quarter of an inch below the outer surface you may find a thin bright-green line. Algae. They are growing within the rock, in the tiny spaces between the individual grains. The quartz of which the grains are composed is sufficiently pellucid to transmit just enough of the sun's rays to enable the tiny plants, on a good summer day, to manufacture food and reproduce.

Other algae manage to exist in the snow itself. They live in a similar way between the individual flakes just below the surface. Their chlorophyll is masked by a red pigment. This protection against damaging ultra-violet rays is more important for them than for the sandstone algae, for sunlight shines more strongly through snow than it does through quartz. During the summer, the sun is warm enough to cause a slight melting of the surface layers, and this provides the algae with the liquid water they need. Dust, brought by the wind, supplies the necessary minerals. The algae themselves manufacture a kind of anti-freeze which keeps the contents of their bodies liquid even when the temperature of the snow falls to several degrees below zero. During the winter, the tiny cells remain largely invisible some distance below the surface, but when summer comes, they propel themselves with microscopic beating

△
Red algae staining the snows of Antarctica

hairs and move up towards the surface, the light and the warmth. So in summer, some parts of the snow fields of both the Arctic and the Antarctic blush pink.

◇

The physical situation at the other end of the earth, in the Arctic, is rather different. The North Pole itself is not covered by land but by the sea. The surface waters are frozen, but beneath this roof of ice swims a rich community of fish. And whereas in the south, the Antarctic continent is encircled and cut off from the rest of the lands of the world by the wide, gale-torn Southern Ocean, in the north, the continents of Europe, Asia and North America all extend for several hundred miles across the Arctic Circle towards the Pole. So plants, together with animals, and indeed human beings, have been able to reach these regions without crossing open water.

Many have done so. A million years ago, during the Ice Age, great ice-caps covered all these northern lands and came as far south as the middle of the British Isles. But as the ice slowly retreated, so plants moved northwards to occupy the land it exposed, and today there are significant communities of animals and plants well north

of the Arctic Circle. As they colonised these new territories, they evolved into somewhat different forms, better adapted to their new circumstances. A species of willow developed that does not grow vertically upwards, like its European and American relatives. To do so would be to risk being flattened by the ferocious Arctic wind. Instead, it grows horizontally, keeping close to the ground. Even in the most favourable circumstances it seldom exceeds four inches in height. But it may become as long as some of its southern relatives are tall. When you walk across a carpet of such prostrate trees, you are, in effect, walking over a woodland canopy.

▷
Arctic poppies and (left) willowherb bloom briefly in the short summer of the high Arctic

◁
The Arctic willow escapes the crippling wind blowing across the tundra by never rising more than an inch or so above the ground. Behind, mountain avens flowers

During the brief summer, Arctic plants have all four of their essentials in reasonable supply. The temperature rises well above freezing and there is liquid water in abundance. Although deep down the ground remains frozen as it has been since the Ice Age, the surface of the glaciers and the snow fields begin to melt and streams and rivers flow across the land. The sun circles around the horizon and does not drop beneath it for weeks on end. As it moves, the flower of the Arctic poppy follows it around so that the flower always faces the sun, soaking up its heat. Nutrients and minerals, however, are in short supply. The rocks, shattered by frost and ground down to a coarse flour by the glaciers, have not yet weathered and been turned into the minerals that can be readily absorbed by the plants. The richest source of nutriment to be found are the dead bodies of the few animals that live up here. There are arctic hares, some birds and, biggest of all, musk ox. When one of these dies, it provides a banquet for plants. Seeds, blown by the wind, are caught in the dome of the huge skull and the cavern of its empty chest. Beneath the remains, the gravelly ground is enriched with nutrients from the animal's decaying flesh. So the open grave of a musk ox becomes the nursery for a rich variety of seedlings which, once they have got a start, may establish a small garden as a permanent memorial to the animal whose death founded them.

Mosquitos swarm in summer but other larger insects that normally live longer than a few days face great difficulties. One species of moth has had to slow down its growth to an almost lichen-like speed. There are so few days in the year when it is warm enough for its caterpillar to feed that it needs sixteen years to grow sufficiently large to pupate. Then, when its seventeenth summer is at its warmest, the adult emerges and looks for a mate. Its food reserves are so meagre that it can only fly for about a fortnight. If it does not breed within that time it will die without leaving any progeny.

The bones of a musk ox provide plants with welcome shelter from the wind, and the nutrients from its decayed flesh, impregnating the soil, supply them with food
▽

The scarcity of such large insects poses a problem for the plants. Those of them which in more southerly lands used insects to transport their pollen, here have to find other means. A little species of mustard has changed its tactics for this reason and now uses the wind, of which there is no shortage. But it still produces its tiny yellow flowers in groups of four, that are so small that the quartet is no bigger than the head of a match, and continues to proclaim its presence to insect couriers, even though there may be none to answer its call.

◇

Purple saxifrage, whose name means stone-breaker, manages to grow on mountain peaks in the narrowest cracks in the rock. Pyrenees
▽

Farther south, in Europe, the severities of the Arctic are only equalled on high mountains. Here in winter, it can also become so cold that plant growth of any kind is brought to a standstill. But when spring comes, the sun climbs higher in the sky than ever it does in the Arctic, temperatures rise to sweltering levels and plants, even at high altitudes, are able to flourish.

Close to the edge of permanent snow, this growing period may be very brief indeed. The snow may have taken so long to melt that

the sun has already passed its summer peak before the rocky cliffs are exposed and there is moisture to be extracted from the gritty ground.

This is where the alpine snowbell grows. Because growing time is so short, it has to be prepared to take immediate advantage of the first thaw. Accordingly, it has, ready and waiting, flower buds that were developed at the end of the previous short summer. Throughout the winter they have remained dormant, protected by the blanket of snow above. In spring, even before the snow melts, the glimmer of slightly brighter light, filtering through the white blanket above, triggers the plant into activity. The dark surface of the flower-buds absorbs the heat of such sunlight that manages to filter down to them and this speeds the melting of the snow. As moisture from the sun-warmed surface of the snow begins to trickle into the ground, the little snowbells suddenly appear in the sunshine, each sitting in the centre of its own dimple in the snow-field.

The alpine snowbell appears in spring high on Alpine peaks even before the snow around it has melted
▽

△
The edelweiss which grows at high altitudes in the Alps protects itself from the cold with a silky fur

More insects fly in the Alps than do in the Arctic, but even so their number is few. It is therefore particularly important for the plants that those insects which do arrive spend the minimum of their time and energy in searching for flowers. Far better that they find them immediately among the rocks and snow and get on with their duties, collecting and delivering pollen. So the tiny Alpine plants, such as the purple saxifrage and the snow gentian produce blossoms that are not only brilliantly coloured, but very large for the size of the plant that bears them. Many help to sustain the insects on their high-altitude forays by producing tubular flowers which can provide their partners with valuable shelter. The dark colour of the flower absorbs the heat of the sun, so inside, out of the wind, there is warmth as well as a reviving swig of nectar.

Cold remains a major danger, for the temperature even in summer may fall well below freezing at night. A furry blanket can help to keep off the worst chills. The edelweiss, growing in cracks in rocks, protects itself with a coat of woolly hairs that gives its leaves and the bracts surrounding its tiny flowers a felt-like appearance.

A Himalayan plant, saussurea, has taken this kind of thermal lagging to extremes. In some species it is difficult to distinguish the leaves within the mound of fur with which they surround themselves. There is a hole in the top which allows pollinating bees to enter and reach the flowers. Inside it is so snug that the insects often overnight there.

Other plants deal with cold by packing their stems tightly together into a cushion. By doing so, the plant creates a miniature ecosystem where the resources of warmth, humidity and nourishment are significantly better than in the world outside it. The cushion's furry exterior acts like a muff, helping to hold any warmth it might contain. The plant may even add to that by, on occasion, expending a little of its food reserves in slightly raising the internal temperature. The sheer bulk of fibres of the cushion retains water like a sponge and the fierce winds do not dry it out. Nor is the nutriment embodied in the leaves lost when they die. Instead of being shed, they remain within the cushion and the upper part of the stems puts out lateral rootlets to reabsorb much of the leaves' constituents just as soon as decay releases them.

No plants develop bigger cushions than those growing on the tops of the mountains in Tasmania. They have a particular need to do so. Snow seldom falls on these peaks because the surrounding sea keeps the climate relatively mild. But the sea does nothing to reduce the wind, and the chill it brings at these altitudes can be very bitter indeed. The plants in winter, lacking a protective blanket of snow, are thus subject to particularly severe chilling.

The plants that form the cushions here belong to the same family as daisies and dandelions, but their flowers are tiny and their stems are packed tightly together. A single square yard may contain a hundred thousand shoots so that a big cushion could easily contain a million stems. They create a landscape of extraordinary beauty, like the exquisitely planned moss garden of a Japanese temple. Rivulets of glassy water trickle between swelling pillows of piercing emerald green. Some cushions are twelve feet across and spill over boulders and around the boles of trees. They may contain several species intermingled so that their surface is spangled with different shades of green.

◁
Saussurea is so woolly that its true character is difficult to see. It is, in fact, a member of the daisy family

△
*Each of the
Tasmanian
cushions may
contain several
different species of
plant which, packed
tightly together,
give it a mottled
surface*

These cushions look so plump and lush that it seems as if your foot would sink up to the ankle if you trod on them. In fact, they are dense and hard and you can walk over them without making so much as a dent if you are careful. A really vigorous stamp would certainly break their surface and this would inflict serious damage for the continuity of their outer surface would no longer be complete. Rain and wind would then penetrate their enclosed world. Nutrients would wash out and heat be lost. Such a wound might well be lethal for the growth of the cushion plants is so slow that they might not able to heal it before they were killed by the cold.

◇

◁
*The largest cushion
plants in the world,
in the mountains of
Tasmania*

*Giant groundsels
growing at 14,000
feet on Mount
Kenya*
▷ ▷

The plants on Mount Kenya, in protecting themselves from cold have also developed into extraordinary shapes and forms – but very different ones. The mountain which rises to over sixteen thousand feet, stands exactly on the equator. This gives the plants a double problem. Not only do they have to withstand freezing temperatures during the night, but during the day they are baked by the equatorial sun blazing down upon them through the thin atmosphere. It is as though the weather shifts from deep winter to high summer and back again every twenty four hours.

The sodden ground during the day seems an excellent site for mosses. And they do indeed grow here. But as soon as night falls, the water in the soil freezes. Ice crystals form in it so quickly that the soil churns up and the mosses cannot retain any hold on the ground. Instead they form balls that are blown around by the wind.

Groundsels also grow here. They are relatives of the dandelions and ragworts that flourish as small yellow-flowered weeds in European gardens. On Mount Kenya, they have evolved into giants. One grows into a tree up to thirty feet tall. Each of its branches ends in a dense rosette of large robust leaves. As the branches grow, so each year the lower ring of leaves in the rosette turn yellow and die. But they are not shed. Instead, they remain attached and form a thick lagging around the trunk. This is of crucial importance to the groundsel. The living leaves in the rosette contain special substances that prevent frost damage to the tissues and even though they may become covered by hoar frost during the night, they thaw out rapidly in the powerful warmth of the morning sun. But then the water within them starts to evaporate through their pores. If the liquid in the supply pipes running up through the trunk were to have frozen during the night, then the leaves would now be unable to replace their water and they would be baked dry and killed. The lagging of the dead leaves, however, prevents the pipes within the trunk from freezing and that particular danger is averted.

The solution, however, generates another problem – this time a nutritional one. Retaining the dead leaves on the trunk prevents the nutrients in them from being released into the soil where they could be reclaimed by the roots. The giant tree-groundsel overcomes that difficulty in the same way as the giant cushion plant of Tasmania. It sprouts rootlets from the side of the trunk which thrust their way into the lagging and extract what nutriment remains there.

A second kind of giant groundsel, growing in slightly moister places, carries its leaves at ground level so that its rosettes look like giant cabbages. They guard their central buds from the frost by folding their leaves over each night. The outer leaves will be frozen, but they, like those of their tree-forming relatives, can withstand that and the tender terminal bud, which cannot, is safe within their tight embrace.

△
Cabbage groundsels, closed for the night. Mount Kenya

There are also two species of lobelia on the upper slopes of the mountain. Both form giant rosettes of leaves on the ground. They are in just as much danger of having their terminal buds frost-bitten as the cabbage groundsel and one of them takes the same preventative measures, folding its leaves over the terminal buds each night.

The other surprisingly does not do this. Instead it remains wide-spread throughout the night. But it has a most ingenious defence.

Its rosette forms a deep watertight cup that contains up to three quarters of a gallon of liquid. Each night, a plate of ice forms across its surface. This acts as a shield, preventing the frost from penetrating more deeply into the pond. The water beneath remains liquid and therefore above freezing point and the submerged bud survives undamaged. It is a minimal defence. Were the nights to last a few hours longer or the temperature to stay below zero during the day, then the contents of the ponds might freeze solid right to the bottom and the bud would be killed. As it is, however, the sun returns after a few hours and all is well.

But now the lobelia faces a different hazard. If the sun shines so hotly during the day that the water in the pond evaporates, then the lobelia would be defenceless when night fell. However, this does not happen. The fluid in the pond is not rain water. Indeed it cannot be for very little rain falls on these slopes. The plant has secreted it from special glands and it contains a slime that hinders evaporation. So even during the hottest afternoons, its defence does not vanish.

The lobelias carry their flowers densely packed around a thick stem that rises from the centre of the rosette. The action of one species in folding its leaves over the bud at night also provides considerable protection for the flowers. But the lobelia species that remains open must have some additional device. In any case, its flowers would be far beyond the reach of its leaves for they are produced around a column that rises several feet high. It protects them in the same way as the tree-groundsel protects the sap in its trunk – with lagging, and it uses not dead leaves but exceptionally long hair-like bracts which grow around each flower and together forms a thick fur around the pillar. The flowers themselves are much shorter than the bracts and are almost hidden by them so that the sunbirds, which pollinate the flowers, have to thrust their heads deeply into the fur to find nectar.

◁
A sunbird searches for a way through a lobelia's fur in order to drink nectar from its flowers

But all the survival strategies of Mount Kenya's plants are still not fully understood. Why should they have evolved in the opposite way to Alpine plants and instead of becoming pygmies have turned into giants? We do not yet know.

△
The bare sun-roasted rocks of the Namib Desert

A thousand miles south of Mount Kenya and, more significantly, fourteen thousand feet lower, lie some of the harshest deserts in the world. So few plants can grow in them that vast areas are covered by bare sand dunes and pavements of gravel and pebbles. To exist here plants have to gather every molecule of water that comes within their reach and develop structures to store it so that it will sustain them through long periods of unrelieved drought.

The Namib Desert, along the south-western coast, may get no more than four inches of rain in a whole year. It is so hot that the surface of outcropping granite develops cracks and ultimately disintegrates into its component crystals. Winds when they come, hurl the fragments back at the rock faces scooping them into bowls, chiselling them into knife-edged towers. But such winds bring no relief to the traveller for they are as hot as the breath from an oven.

The Namib close to the coast does, however, have one source of moisture that most deserts lack. Almost every day, a fog rolls in from the sea, billowing across the dunes. On slopes where little else can survive, a lichen grows in a great orange carpet. It forms not thin blisters on rocks but bushy structures several inches high. The fog condenses into droplets that hang on the wiry tangled branches and are swiftly absorbed by the fungal partner before the sun is strong enough to evaporate them. The quantity of water captured is minuscule but it is sufficient to enable the algae, held within the fungal threads, to photosynthesise.

Pebble plants grow in the stonier patches of the same desert. They survive by living partly underground. Their leaves have been reduced to a single pair, fat, round and succulent, with just a groove between them from which, in the right season, will sprout a surprisingly large flower. Such a rounded shape, with a very low surface area for a given volume, reduces evaporation to a minimum and is therefore a great help to the plant in conserving its water in the intense heat. But as has been noted earlier it may bring an additional benefit. Outside the flowering season, the plant is very difficult to find among the gravel and pebbles, so its shape could also serve as a defence against detection by grazing animals – ostriches and tortoises, porcupines and perhaps a few gerbils. That possibility is supported by the fact that, to a remarkable degree, the colour of these plants varies to match that of the surrounding pebbles. Some are grey or blue; others yellow, orange or brown. In places where there is an outcrop of quartz, they may be milky white. While searching for them, you may find instead what looks, at first sight, to be a fragment of an ancient mosaic pavement, a group of button-sized discs fitting closely together, each a pellucid flinty grey elegantly rimmed with red. Blow hard on them and the sand disperses to reveal that these are the flat tops of a group of rod-like pillars, several inches long. They are, in fact, leaves and this is a window plant.

When the plant first germinates, it puts down a short but muscular root. Having got a grip on the surrounding soil, it contracts, pulling down its terminal bud below ground level The leaves that sprout from it are thick and succulent and absorb moisture as soon as it becomes available. Keeping cool below the surface they are well placed to do that. They are not so well placed to photosynthesise since only their tips are in the light. But those tips are not only flat but translucent. The sunlight falling on them passes through them and then down a series of aligned transparent crystals of oxalic acid

running down the centre of the pillar until it reaches the grains of chlorophyll that are distributed internally around the sides and the bottom of the leaf. The reddish rims, that surround the leaf-tops and give them such subtle beauty, disappear when window plants are grown in cultivation outside a desert. It is apparently a defensive pigmentation, like our sun-tan, and only develops when the sun is particularly ferocious. Nor, in cultivation, do the plants keep their leaves buried. Released from the stresses of the desert, they sprout several inches high above the surface. Like many another desert dweller, release from the rigours and disciplines of their desert home greatly changes their character.

▷
Welwitschia grows in scattered groups along a strip of de-sert 600 miles long and 125 miles wide in south-western Africa

◁
Only the tops of the leaves of the window plant are visible. The main body of the plant is below ground, out of the worst of the heat. Namibia

Further inland, one of the oddest of all plants manages to survive largely on dew. Welwitschia is related to the conifers and the cycads and consists of just two long strap-like leaves that sprout from a central swollen trunk only a few inches high. The leaves grow continuously from their base and become very long indeed. They would doubtless be even longer were it not for the desert winds which, blowing them back and forth, frays the ends into tatters. Even as it is, these leaves may be twenty yards long and lie curled in untidy heaps around the stunted trunk. They collect droplets of dew and channel them down runnels into the ground where the water is absorbed and stored in an immense conical tap root.

Swollen roots are used by a great number of plants as storage tanks. Beneath the sand, they are out of sight and not easily found by thirsty animals living on the surface. Hottentot bread is the name given to a yam that develops an immense underground tuber that may weigh as much as seven hundred pounds and fully justifies its specific name of elephantipes – elephant foot. Every desert – in Australia and South America, in the Sahara, the Gobi and Madagascar – has such plants. And in every one, an ability to recognise the leaf of a tiny sprig standing unobtrusively in the sand as an indication of a buried water store was once the traditional life-saving knowledge of nomadic people.

But there are also other methods of storage. The quiver tree that grows in the Namib is a kind of aloe. Like the rest of its family, it has thick succulent leaves growing in a rosette, but these are hoisted twenty feet in the air, each at the end of a stumpy branch. That in itself is a way of escaping the worst of the devastating heat and reducing the amount of moisture inevitably lost by evaporation from the surface of their leaves. The branches themselves are thickly covered in a fine white powder. That too helps in keeping cool for it reflects the sun's heat instead of absorbing it.

The branches and trunk are filled with a soft fibre that can hold a great quantity of water. This inner tissue, which is too soft to be called wood, is easily cleaned out. The Bushmen who once lived in this desert used to do that. They then fitted the resultant tube with a little leather cap, top and bottom, and used it as a container for their arrows, which is why the tree is called a quiver tree. But if a drought is really severe, the tree has to take even more extreme measures to prevent the loss of the water. Leaves must have at least a few pores in their surface to allow the exchange of gases that is an essential part of food manufacture. Their mere existence risks water loss. So in extreme circumstances, the quiver tree amputates itself. A branch, at a point immediately below the terminal rosette, will constrict and become so thin that the whole rosette drops off. The stump then seals itself, so protecting more effectively the water within it. Such amputated limbs can never regrow their leaves. Their essential terminal buds have been lost. But other rosettes remain and in this reduced form the tree may retain enough water during the drought to survive until the rains at last bring relief.

◁
Pachypodium, from the deserts of Madagascar, stores water in its swollen stump-like trunk

Quiver trees shed the ends of some of their branches and are so able to endure the most severe droughts. Namibia
▷ ▷

The half-mens, growing in the same desert, has reduced its leaves to one small bunch sprouting from the top of a pillar-like trunk bristling all over with ranks of long spines that must deter many a thirsty animal from gnawing it in search of the liquid it contains. It owes its odd name to a Hottentot myth that claims that the plant is half-way to being human and indeed these austere prickly pillars, crested with a bunch of crinkly leathery leaves, do have an eerie humanoid appearance. The rings that encircle the trunk up its length, like concentric rings within the trunk of an oak tree, are said each to represent one year's growth. If that is so, then many of the half-mens must be several centuries old.

On the ground around them grow numerous fat, spiny leafless plants that any non-botanist could be forgiven for calling – without hesitation and even perhaps a certain amount of pride in his expertise – cacti. Only if they are in flower might you suspect that they are not. Then a botanist would notice that the numbers of petals and anthers are quite different from those of cacti. These are euphorbias, members of one of the largest of all families of flowering plants with over seven thousand species. In Europe, its common

The half-mens from south-western Africa only produces leaves from the very top of its spine-covered stem and sheds them during the height of summer ▽

*△ and ▽
American cacti
(above and below
left) and African
euphorbias (above
and below right)
in similar
conditions may
closely resemble one
another*

representatives are dog's mercury and spurge. In South America, euphorbias grow into trees and shrubs, among them the rubber tree and the manioc plant. In African forests, its members include the castor oil bush. And in African deserts they become cacti look-alikes.

The cactus family is, in fact, exclusively American, with hundreds of different species growing in deserts from Canada to Chile. The reason that members of these two families resemble one another so

closely is that similar conditions of heat and drought have stimulated the same physical response. Both abandon their leaves at an early stage, since these inevitably lose a great deal of water, and both carry out their photosynthesis under the hard waxy surface of their stems which are green with chlorophyll. Both store water in a bloated pillar-like trunk. And both defend that water from robbers by armouring their trunks with sharp spines.

The ability of cacti to absorb water is spectacular. In severe droughts, they may lose as much as twenty percent of their liquid. Their bodies become shrivelled and thin. But when the rain does fall, they suck it up with great speed. Many have deep pleats running vertically up their stems. These expand like the bellows of an accordion as the stem fills. They must be counted the most successful of desert-livers, for one of their number, the prickly pear, has been introduced into deserts outside the Americas – in Australia, Africa and the Mediterranean – and has colonised those arid lands so successfully that it has become a rampant pest, crowding out other native species.

◇

◁

White Namaqualand daisies, orange ursinias and purple mesembryanthemums bloom beneath quiver trees in the deserts of south-western Africa

South of the Namib desert, lies Namaqualand. Here there is just a little more rain and it falls with marginally greater reliability. Droughts can still be so severe that during the dry season great areas seem to be bare of plant life. But that is illusory. Dig and you will find an astonishing abundance of bulbs and corms. The leaves of the plants that produced and stocked them shrivelled and died at the beginning of summer and now have largely disappeared. The number of these dormant vegetable stores is almost unbelievable. So abundant are they that the various species have to operate a tier system, each occupying its own preferred depth beneath the surface. In some areas, there may be as many as ten thousand in the earth just below one square metre of land surface.

Nor are bulbs and corms the only forms of life asleep in the sand. Sieving it will reveal seeds. These came from plants that had condensed their entire lives into a few weeks. In that short time they grew, put out leaves, manufactured food, flowered and set seed.

Springtime in Namaqualand
▷▷

Some of the seeds may have been shed at the end of the last season. Others may be considerably older, for many species load the coats of their seeds with a chemical inhibitor. Until a shower of rain washes that away, there will be no germination. This practice ensures that the seeds will not be brought to life by an isolated shower of rain, only to die when the desert rapidly dries and the drought reasserts its grip. There has to be a prolonged soaking, and therefore a reasonable prospect of available moisture for a sustained period, before they will germinate and put their lives at risk.

Southern Africa is the headquarters of a vast and varied family, the mesembryanthemums. Its members include the pebble-plant and the window-plant of the Namib, but in Namaqualand there is enough annual rain to allow them to grow their leaves in a more normal way. They must nonetheless guard against drought and they also do so by storing water in their leaves which, though more conventionally shaped, are still thick and fleshy. One species retains liquid in tiny bladders on the surface of each bloated leaf that glisten in the sunshine and so give it the name, apt though improbable in these sun-baked lands, of 'ice plant'.

Most of the Namaqualand mesems, as they are known for short, do not scatter their seeds after flowering but retain them in capsules. The structure of these devices is usually very intricate indeed. When the first rain falls, perhaps as a short and isolated shower, the capsules absorb moisture and swell, causing a star-shaped set of valves to open. But even now the seeds are not shed. That must wait for a second shower. Then a raindrop striking a valve operates a mechanism that flings out the seeds for a distance of yards.

There is still a chance that the rain may not last long enough to sustain the seedlings and that they will die soon after they have germinated. Some mesems take out an insurance against even that possibility. They keep a small proportion of their seeds locked away in a compartment that no amount of raindrops can dislodge. These will only be released months, if not years later when the whole capsule has finally decayed. Then they take their chance with the rest of the seeds in the sandy ground.

When the rains do come, the adult plants burst into flower again. The cumbersome name mesembryanthemum means 'mid-day flower', for they only open their daisy-like blooms to their fullest

△
Sturt's pea blooms
after the rain in the
deserts of Australia

extent during the middle of the day. As the sun climbs, so the colour of their carpets intensifies. As the season progresses, gladioli, freesias and amaryllis rise from the bulbs and corms. Daisies and poppies sprout from seeds. For a few brief weeks, if conditions are favourable, the desert is covered with sheets of blue, white, yellow and red. But then the merciless sun shrivels the blooms and the sand is exposed once more.

◇

So plants, by a variety of stratagems, solve the problem of surviving in places where only a minimum of moisture is available during only a brief part of the year. But heavy daily drenchings the year round can equally, in some circumstances, cause problems.

In the north-east corner of South America, where Venezuela, Guyana and Brazil all meet, stands a group of huge rectangular plateaux called, locally, tepuis. Their flat tops rise above the clouds. Their sheer walls are naked rock striped by the white vertical lines of waterfalls, among them the tallest in the world. Some of these

Roraima, the Lost
World of Venezuela
▷▷

cascades are so high that the wind carries their waters away as droplets before they can reach the ground.

The biggest and most famous of these tepuis is Roraima, nine thousand feet tall, ten miles long, up to three miles wide and encircled by precipices. It is often called, with some justice, the Lost World.

The first European travellers to explore this region in the sixteenth century, brought back stories of an impregnable mountain that stood like a gigantic fortress in the country around the headwaters of the Orinoco. Later explorers, when they saw it, marvelled at its austere geometric shape and speculated on what might live on its flat summit. Most accepted that they would never find out because the mountain was unclimbable. It was not until 1884 that a British botanist, Everard Im Thurn, finally managed to find a way up a huge sloping ledge on its north-west flank and reach the top. His lecture in London about his achievement caused great excitement. One of his listeners was the novelist, Arthur Conan Doyle. Although Im Thurn had not found any spectacular new species of animal on the summit plateau, Conan Doyle's imagination was sufficiently stirred for him to speculate that if dinosaurs had survived anywhere on earth, it might be in such a place. In 1912, he put his fantasies into a novel he called *The Lost World* and Roraima has been linked with that title ever since.

In fact the mountain does contain species that are found nowhere else on earth. But they are not antique survivors from long past geological eras. They are new species which, isolated on the summit plateau and drenched by one of the heaviest rainfalls anywhere on earth, have had to evolve special abilities in order to survive.

The rock of which Roraima is composed is a hard and very ancient quartzite. It has been sculpted into grotesquely extravagant shapes. There are stone mushrooms thirty feet high, teetering on tiny bases so constricted that it seems as if the slightest push would make them topple; dense ranks of columns that might be the roofless ruins of a temple; windows and archways; pagodas, towers and minarets; cromlechs, dolmens and castellations. Here and there, chasms a hundred feet deep and too wide to leap across, unexpectedly slice through the rocks. Occasionally vertical walls are undercut at their foot to form caves – places to be noted for the time when

The contorted black-ened rocks on Roraima's summit

the heavy rain becomes intolerably chilling and the route back through the rocky labyrinths to a tent proves undiscoverable.

Shapes like these are very reminiscent of rocks in the Namib. They must surely, like them, have been roasted into disintegration by the sun and carved by the wind. But that must have been during an earlier era, for no such winds blow across the summit these days. Confirmation that the processes of erosion, whatever they were, are no longer at work comes from the surface of the rocks. They are black. At least, they appear to be. But when you examine the bed of a stream, or even turn over a loose boulder, you discover that the quartzite is actually pinkish white. The black comes from a super-ficial skin. It is produced by algae. Their extensive coating of the rock proves that it is no longer being eroded. It also makes clear that these water-swilled rocks of Roraima provide an excellent habitat for such simple plants.

But for more complex ones, life here is very difficult. Rain falls so frequently and heavily that the rocks are perpetually sluiced by water. In flat areas it lies in immense puddles many yards across but only a few inches deep. It spouts from cracks and gurgles through gullies. Only in a few places are the rocks contoured into

◁

The recently eroded cliffs of Roraima are pink, showing that their blackness else-where is an algal skin. Larger plants manage to grow in the gravel filled cracks

shapes that can retain sufficient gravel and sand to enable a plant to root. And even where there is some semblance of earth, it is very poor in the soluble nutrients that a more mature soil would provide. Plants must, therefore, have additional ways of finding food.

Orchids are particularly well-equipped for coping with such im-poverished environments, for they are helped by the mycorrhizal fungi around their roots. So they have less problems than most and they flourish in considerable numbers on the tepuis. Roraima alone has at least thirty different species.

Sundews, which elsewhere in the world live in bogs and nutri-ent-poor soils also do well. And the tepuis are the only home today of the marsh pitchers. If it is true that they represent the earliest, most primitive members of the carnivorous pitcher-plant family, then perhaps they may have survived up here because they have been isolated from other evolutionary developments in the wider world below. Maybe Conan Doyle was more correct than he knew.

A species of sun-dew, unique to Mount Roraima
▽

Bladderworts also thrive here. They are water plants found in wetlands in many parts of the world, including Britain, and they are

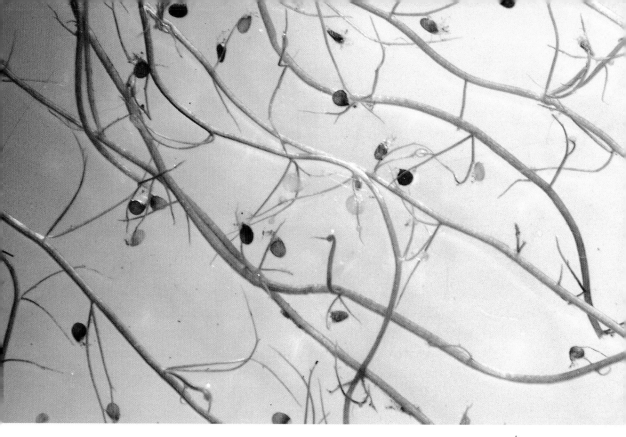

△

The green capsules of bladderwort are traps awaiting their victims. Those that are black have recently made a catch

so successful in trapping animals that they do not grow roots of any kind. Their traps, the bladders from which they get their name, are tiny transparent capsules. Glands on the inner surface of these are able to absorb water, and in doing so create a partial vacuum within. Each has a tiny door fringed with sensitive bristles. If a small water creature, such as a mosquito larva, touches one of these, the bristle acts as a lever, slightly distorting the edge of the door so that it no longer fits tightly on the rim. Water rushes in, sweeping the door inwards and with it, the little organism that touched the hair. The swirl of water within the capsule pushes the door back again and the prey is imprisoned. The whole action is completed within a fraction of a second. Once again, the glands start to suck out the water. Another set secretes digestive acids and the captive is killed, dissolved and consumed. The bladderwort has fed. Within two hours, the bladder's partial vacuum has been restored and the trap is reset.

Several species of bladderworts flourish on the tepuis, growing not only in pools but also on water-logged ground as they do elsewhere in the world. But Roraima has a carnivorous plant all of its own. Bromeliads grow abundantly in the forests around the base

△
An adult waterflea,
approaching a
bladderwort's trap,
is probably big
enough to be safe

of the tepuis, their miniature ponds providing a refuge for a varied population of small animals just as those of most members of the family do. But up on the summit of Roraima, food is in such short supply that one species of bromeliad has adopted the practice established by the marsh pitcher. It has developed glands in the walls of its vase which absorb nutriment from the dead bodies of its lodgers. Whether it has yet the ability to kill them has not been established. Even if it has not, its animal inhabitants are still at hazard. A bladderwort has invaded these vegetable ponds, searching for prey. It moves from one bromeliad to another by extending a tendril over the leaves of the rosette and out across the rocks. Up on the nutrient-poor rocks of Roraima, there are carnivores lying in wait – even inside other carnivores.

The plants of the tepuis, adapted to their cold wet conditions, cannot survive in the warm savannahs and forests three thousand feet below from which their ancestors must have come. They are in effect imprisoned on islands. Evolution proceeds particularly swiftly in small self-contained communities, for genetic variations appearing in an individual are less likely to be swamped and lost than they are in bigger populations. So the tepuis today have developed a unique flora. At least half of the species of plants living on their summits are now unique. The plateaux, between them, have five species of pitchers, seven sundews and nine hundred species of orchid, all of which grow nowhere else. Many are restricted to the single summit on which they evolved. The tepuis are the Galapagos of the floral world.

A plant living in fresh water is likely to have three of its four vital essentials in some abundance. Liquid water is all around; nutrients are freely available in most lakes and rivers for they are swept into them from the surrounding land; and although the surface of a river may freeze over during winter, it is only the shallowest streams and lakes in the most bitterly cold weather that are liable to freeze solid. Indeed, water plants may survive in winter when those on the banks beside them are killed by frost. Only one of the four essential requirements presents problems for them – light.

In still or slowly-moving waters there is one easy way to collect it: a plant can float its leaves upon the surface. No plant does this on a more spectacular scale or more aggressively than the giant Amazon water-lily. A leaf first appears on the surface as a huge fat bud, studded with spines. Within a few hours, it bursts open and

The leaf-bud of the giant Amazon water lily expands swiftly, pushing aside its rivals
▽

△
The Amazon water-lily produces leaves that are so big and numerous that it dominates the waters where it grows

starts to spread. Its margin has an up-turned rim, six inches high, so that as it expands it is able to shoulder aside any other floating leaf that gets in its way. Beneath, it is strengthened with girder-like ribs which make the whole structure rigid. They also contain air-spaces within them that keep it afloat. Expanding at the rate of half a square yard in a single day, the leaf grows until it is six feet across. The underside of the leaf is a rich purple colour and armoured with abundant sharp spikes, perhaps as a defence against leaf-eating fish. One plant can produce forty or fifty of such leaves in a single growing season and monopolise the surface so effectively that few plants of other kinds can grow alongside or below it.

The first specimen of this magnificent water-lily to reach Europe was brought back to London by Sir Robert Schomburgk in 1837. Unhappily, it died on the way, but even its preserved remains caused a sensation. It was awarded a genus of its own and named Victoria in honour of the Queen. In 1847, viable seeds did arrive at Kew and there the gardeners managed to get them to germinate. One of the seedlings was sent to Joseph Paxton who was in charge of the Duke of Devonshire's splendid gardens at Chatsworth. He built a special house for it containing a pond where the water was

△
The virginal white flower of the Amazon lily on the first evening it opens

kept at tepid temperatures matching those of its native Amazon. It put out its gigantic leaves and eventually, to the amazement of the gardening world, it flowered.

Paxton was not only a gardener of great skill but an architect of near-genius. He built one of the first big glasshouses. When he came to design the cast-iron supports for his hitherto unprecedented expanse of glass, he remembered the ribs and struts of his giant water-lily that supported the gigantic leaves and used them as the basis of his designs not only for the glass-houses at Chatsworth but also, a few years later, for his architectural masterpiece, the Crystal Palace in London. He also established a custom that has become almost obligatory ever since for those who wish to demonstrate the size and strength of the lily's leaves. He persuaded his small daughter Annie to pose for pictures, sitting on one.

The Amazon water-lily is able to produce such large and strong structures because it can collect an abundance of food through its roots from the mud at the bottom of the lake. But roots need to breathe and the mud at the bottom of Amazonian swamps and

A beetle, after being imprisoned for twenty-four hours, leaves the fertilised lily flower with a load of pollen and seeks another white one

pools contains little or no oxygen. The lily, however, pipes air down to them through tubes running down the long stems of the leaves, which may be as much as 35 feet long.

The lily's flower, like its leaves, is outsize – a foot and a quarter across. It opens for the first time in the evening. Its multiple petals are pure white and consequently very conspicuous in the darkness. It draws attention to itself with a rich perfume that a particular species of beetle finds irresistible. They fly over the water and settle on the flowers in large numbers. And they find a rich reward. The flower has, in its centre, a circle of small knobs that are full of sugar and starch and the beetles feast on them greedily. While they do so, the flower's petals slowly close over them and hold them captive for the whole night. As they continue to feed in their prison, so the lily's anthers ripen and begin to shed pollen. The flower retains its captives throughout the next day, but when night falls for the second time, it opens once again. Now it has turned pink. The beetles, sticky with the remains of their banquet, are also smeared with pollen. And away they fly to find another food-laden lily flower.

The nearest, of course, are others springing from the same plant. If the beetles landed on one of these, the plant would have pollinated itself and the value of the beetles' visit negated. But there is no danger of this happening. The beetles are programmed to search for virginal white flowers. All those on the plant this night have turned pink and the beetles fly off to look for more white ones. It will not be until the next day that this lily will produce a fresh crop of white ones, and with them attract a fresh group of beetles.

Water-lilies, spectacular though they are in their many species, are only partially adapted to an aqueous existence. Their leaves collect oxygen and carbon dioxide from the air, and they rely on insects of the air to pollinate them. Other water-living plants have evolved ways of breaking these connections with the outside world and are now much more thorough-going water-dwellers.

Water celery has long narrow flat leaves that remain below the surface and absorb the oxygen and carbon dioxide they need from that dissolved in water around them. It also exploits water in its pollination techniques. Its flowers are either male or female. The female flower opens its three petals while it is still underwater and then rises up towards the surface on a rapidly lengthening stem. The male bud makes the journey even more swiftly. Before it even opens, and while it is still some distance below the surface, it breaks

The water celery sends its female flower up to the surface on a long thin stem
▽

▷
The female flower of the water celery held down by its stem creates a dimple in the surface of the water

off its stem and floats upwards. Once on the surface it unfurls its petals and erects twin stamens. With the stamens serving as sails, this tiny vessel is then wafted across the surface of the water.

The female flower is also blown by the wind but it is anchored by its stem. As the breeze tugs at it, so its stem pulls it lower in the water, creating a dimple in the surface. The male ship, moving freely, sails into the dimple, toboggans down its slope and collides so violently with the female flower that the pollen is knocked out of its anthers. The female flower, having achieved fertilisation, then closes. Its stem tightens into a corkscrew, pulling it back beneath the surface. And there, safely underwater, it develops its seeds.

▷
A flotilla of male water celery flower boats sailing towards the female

Most lakes can only be temporary homes. The rivers that flow into them carry sediment. As they enter a lake's still waters, the sediment sinks to the bottom. Year by year, the lake shallows. Slowly it turns into a swamp. As it does so, land-living plants advance into it from the margins. If they are to be successful, they must establish a firm root-hold. The bigger they are, the more necessary this will be, and the biggest of them all is a conifer, the swamp cypress. Its underwater roots develop tall spikes and vertical flanges like knees that project above the surface of the water. It used to be thought that these structures enabled the roots, groping in the stagnant mud, to collect gaseous oxygen. But no one has been able to demonstrate that there is any gas exchange at their surface. Now it is thought that they serve a different purpose. They catch sediment as it swirls into the lake and cause it to settle around them, so providing the tree with a steadily widening and firmer platform.

◇

The ability to anchor mud and build a solid base is even more valuable where the river finally reaches the sea. Here mud accumulates not only because the river water has slowed down but because, as it meets salty water, the smallest of the particles held in suspension coagulate into an extremely fine-grained, sticky mud. In the tropics, this is where the mangroves grow.

Exploring a mangrove swamp is neither easy nor comfortable. The trees support themselves with numerous arching prop-roots and they grow so close together that these supports form a complex interlacing tangle. As you try to clamber through them, the sharp barnacles and shells with which they are encrusted cut your hands and legs. The mud in which they stand has a peculiarly glutinous quality and if you are not careful you will sink up to your knees in it. The air hangs heavy, humid and hot, for there is seldom any wind. Mosquitos hum and whine. There is a dank smell of decay and a whiff of rotten eggs. Occasionally the shriek of a water bird echoes through the trees and strange plops and clicks come from the muddy surface as the receding waters expose the tunnels of mud-dwellers and their occupants come out to feed.

◁
Swamp cypresses surrounded by their knee-like roots. South Carolina

The humid, tangled world of the mangroves
▷ ▷

But the difficulties faced by a human being are as nothing compared with those with which the mangroves themselves must deal. Twice a day the tide rises to drown their roots, and then recedes to expose them to the air. Twice a day the water around them changes from salty as the tide comes in, to almost fresh as it goes out and the flow of the river water pushes back the sea. And every day, there is the danger that the slightest eddy in the current will remove mud that was deposited only yesterday.

The trees' problem with sea water is due to the fact that when two solutions with differing concentrations of salt come into contact on either side of a membrane, they tend to equalise. So salt will enter the mangrove's root tissues and water within those tissues will flow out into the sea water. Some mangroves deal with this continuous inward flow of salt by carrying it away from their roots in their sap and depositing it in their older leaves that are soon due to be shed. Others have glands on their leaves which excrete it in solutions that are twenty times more concentrated than their sap, and even greater than it is in sea water.

They supply oxygen to their waterlogged roots through special pores in their arching props which are only submerged for brief periods, or in vertical spikes that rise in long lines from roots snaking out just under the surface of the mud.

The aerial prop roots give adult trees considerable stability. But seedlings have more difficulty in getting a hold on the capriciously moving surface of the mud. Some species of mangrove, however, manage to plant their offspring with as much firmness as a gardener armed with a dibble. The seeds germinate while they are still attached to their parent. A long green spike develops that hangs vertically downwards. In some species it may measure as much as two feet. Eventually, it falls. If the tide is out, it may stab straight into the soft mud. Tiny rootlets then grow out from its flanks with great speed and within hours the young seedling may have established itself firmly enough to resist the swill of the returning tide.

If the tide happens to be in when the seedling falls, then instead of rooting immediately, it travels. That may be riskier, for it may be swept out to sea and lost altogether. But potentially it is more beneficial for the species as a whole, for the youngster is taken away from its natal swamp where it would be competing with its parent

▷
The air-breathing roots of the white mangrove. Madagascar

and ferried to territory that may not yet have been colonised by mangroves. At first, it hangs vertically in the brackish water. But if it is carried beyond the estuary then the water becomes saltier and more buoyant so that the seedling begins to float horizontally. That may save its life. If the tender terminal bud, from which leaves will spring in due course, were exposed, unshaded in the tropical sun, it could easily over-heat, even scorch. Floating horizontally, however, it is continually lapped by water and kept cool. The flank of the long root benefits from being exposed along its length for it is green with chlorophyll and is able to photosynthesise. The food it manufactures keeps the whole root alive and growing and it can survive floating at sea for months. If eventually the capricious tides do carry it to another brackish estuary, then the buoyancy of the water is reduced and the young mangrove once again hangs vertically, ready to catch on the bottom of shallows which might be a suitable place to grow.

◁

Mangrove seeds, still attached to their parent, germinate and produce long green spear-like roots. Northern Australia

Mangrove seedlings colonising a vacant stretch of mud. U.S. Virgin Islands
▽

The number of mangrove species is large, but they do not form a single family. They come from several that are not closely related to one another. Just as the challenge of living in a desert has led plants of different families to adopt similar shapes, so the trials of the estuaries have produced a whole group of somewhat similar-looking but unrelated species of tree to which we have given the single name of mangrove.

◇

Where the coast is not muddy but rocky, trees cannot survive. They would soon be smashed by the pounding waves. The only tactic here is to be flexible and ride the thrusts of the waves rather than resist them. And that is what the sea-wracks do. They are algae. Those that live between the tides have to take precautions against being dried out during their twice daily exposure to the air and they do so by covering themselves with a coat of mucus. It is this that makes them so slippery under foot. Some species develop gas-filled bladders in their fronds so that, as the tide sweeps in and out, they rise and fall and remain close to the surface within reach of the all-important light.

Algae being simple plants do not develop flowers. Nor do they have internal vessels to transport their sap. But that does not mean that they cannot achieve great size. They need to grow tall if they are to colonise deep water and yet remain within range of the essential sunlight. And they do. Bull kelp growing around the shores of New Zealand develops a stem as thick as a hawser with a huge gas-filled bladder at the end. Once this reaches the surface of the sea, it puts out an immense floating blade. Similar gigantic growths are found in the ocean off the coasts of Japan and California. These are the high forests of the sea. The longest fronds are nearly two hundred feet tall, which makes them comparable to the trees in a tropical rain forest. And like such forests, they provide homes for a multitude of different creatures. Shoals of fish swoop through them, like flocks of birds; molluscs crawl around their bases; carnivores such as octopus and dragon fish lurk in ambush among their stems.

▷
A forest of giant kelp growing off the coast of southern California

Anchorage of some kind is essential for plants such as these. Without it, they could be washed ashore by the tides and stranded; or, equally damaging, they might be swept by currents into great stacks where only those on the outer margins could get sufficient light or be refreshed by currents. Thus great areas of the ocean, where the sea bed lies thousands of feet below the surface, are closed to them. Only one part of the open ocean is sufficiently still and stagnant to make a floating existence possible for them. That is the centre of the immense eddy that circulates around the Caribbean, the Sargasso Sea. There an alga, closely related to the wracks, accumulates in great rafts. They too have their permanent populations of animals that are specially adapted to the opportunities they offer. Shrimps, crabs and sea-horses clamber around the tangled fronds and small angler fish, camouflaged with little growths of skin that exactly match the colour and shape of the fronds, squat invisibly ready to snap up passers-by.

△
Sargasso weed floating free on the surface of the sea

▷
The inhabitants of a floating world, an angler fish (above) and a Sargasso crab (below)

Most of the surface of the world is covered by salt water; most of it, therefore is beyond the reach of large, highly-evolved flowering plants. The only plants that can flourish here are the simplest of all – floating single-celled algae. Some are enclosed in small plates of cellulose and propel themselves with twin beating threads so they spin like tops. But they are nonetheless capable of purposeful movement. Each has a tiny red spot which is sensitive to light and these great floating shoals move up towards the surface at certain times of the day and seasons of the year. Others extract silica from seawater and secrete for themselves exquisite caskets, perforated and sculpted with the delicacy of Venetian glass. Some float singly, others link together in chains connected by microscopic threads of mucus.

These, perhaps the least considered by humanity of all the plants on the globe, have all four of the essentials for life in abundance. The water around them never drops more than a degree or so below freezing; they are always within the reach of sunlight; and they are constantly provided with nutrients as currents bring up from the deep sea floor the rich ooze created by the decay of the dead bodies of the ocean's inhabitants.

They are the basis of all life in the seas. As they drift in vast clouds, slowly manufacturing food and replicating themselves, microscopic animals, scarcely bigger than they are, consume them. Among these browsers are the larvae of corals and crustaceans, molluscs and fish. This whole community, animal and vegetable, is known as the plankton, the floaters. And the plankton in turn provides food for all the rest of the ocean's inhabitants. Small fish consume it piecemeal. Slightly larger fish take it wholesale, filtering it out with rakers on their gills. Bigger fish are nourished by it second-hand when they eat the smaller fish. And it is sieved from the water in the mouths of the biggest of all fish, the whale shark, as well as the biggest animal of any kind that has ever existed, the blue whale.

And we, together with all other land animals, also depend upon these floating meadows. More than the tropical rain forests, the vast prairies or any other tracts of terrestrial vegetation, they are the main factor in maintaining the balance of gases in the earth's atmosphere. They produce the bulk of the oxygen we breathe.

▷

The pastures of the oceans, floating algae

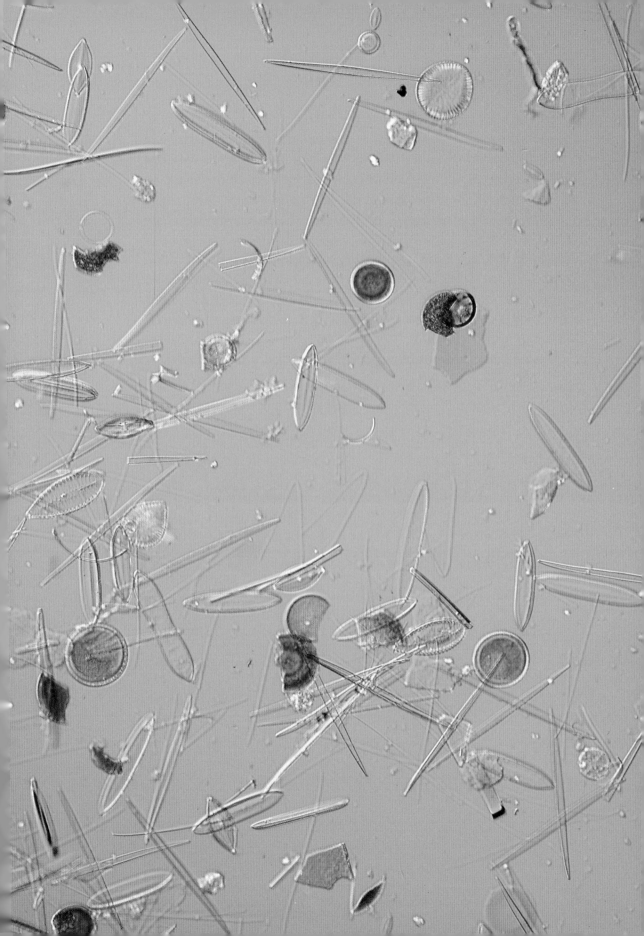

Plants, whether very simple or highly complex, have colonised almost the whole of the surface of our planet, from the snows of the Poles to the lush rain forests on the equator. Some tolerate far harsher circumstances than any animal can. They live in oven-hot conditions where animals can only briefly venture, and survive in extremes of cold that would freeze an animal to death.

Only one thing they cannot survive – the determined onslaughts of humanity. Ever since we appeared on earth as a species, we have dug them up and cut them down, burnt them and poisoned them. Today, we are doing so on a greater scale than ever before. We destroy them at our peril. Without them, neither we, nor any other animal can exist. It is time now for us to cherish our green inheritance, not to pillage it.

Without it we will surely perish.

ACKNOWLEDGMENTS

There may be authors who sit locked away in solitude to produce their works, and they doubtless owe thanks only to those who bring them cups of coffee. This book was certainly not produced that way. Putting the words of the foregoing chapters on paper was only the last stage in a process that began when my television colleagues, Mike Salisbury, Neil Nightingale, Keith Scholey and I came together and decided that plants – as against gardening or ecology – had been much neglected in television and that it was high time that a series of natural history programmes was made in which plants were the heroes and not the victims of the action.

Once BBC Television had accepted the project, Mark Flowers joined us. He took the lead in burrowing through scientific journals, ferreting out stories of which we knew little or nothing but which amplified the main themes which we had already sketched. He drew our attention to many astonishments. More came when Richard Kirby and Tim Shepherd joined the group. Their particular and very rare expertise lies in time-lapse photography. The business of speeding up a plant's actions by exposing a frame of film every minute or every hour or every day, and then transmitting them all at a rate of twenty-five every second may sound simple. But how do you calculate what the frequency of shooting should be; how do you allow for movements by the plants during the night; how do you deal with the vicissitudes of the weather and the wilfulness of plants that are determined to grow in the opposite direction to the one that had been planned for them? And how, after working on a single shot, frame by frame for three months, do you recover your enthusiasm when, just before the action reaches its climax, a sudden gust of unprecedentedly strong wind totally and irredeemably wrecks the subject? My wonder at the sequences Richard and Tim produced is equalled only by my admiration for the resourcefulness and ingenuity that was needed to produce them.

As work progressed over the three years that the programmes

took to make, so the team grew into the one that is listed opposite. All those named there played vital parts in creating the programmes, and therefore contributed invaluably to these pages. I am very grateful indeed to them all.

The whole television team, in turn, became increasingly indebted to our botanical advisers. We consulted them in universities and botanic gardens all over the world, by letter, fax and telephone. All these scientists, without exception, dealt with our enquiries with such patience and sympathy that I have come to believe that botanists, as a genus, are not only kind and gentle but preternaturally tolerant. Were this a scholarly textbook, their names would appear in a bibliography together with the titles of their research papers and those of the academic journals in which they were first published. Such an appendix in a popular work such as this would be out of place and I hope they will forgive me for its absence.

Having discovered from such sources the kind of happenings we wished to film, we then had to venture into the field and find our subjects. Once again, we found guides and advisers wherever we looked. Some were academic botanists, some dedicated amateur naturalists and some had expertise not so much in botany as in ways of getting about difficult country.

Each of us involved in the filming incurred his or her own special debts. I owe them, in particular to Harold Braack, Neil Macgregor, Anton Pauw and Graham Williams in South Africa and William Craig in Kenya; Satoko Nakahara and Professor Utsonomiya in Japan; Dr Peter Attiwell, Dr Steven Hopper and Dr Kingsley Dixon in Australia; Dr Josef Svoboda in the Arctic, Bill Duyck and Dr Robert Griffiths in the United States, and Charles Brewer-Carias in Venezuela; and Anthea and Tony Lamb, Jamili Nais and Elaine Campbell in Sabah. One expedition figures particularly prominently in my memory and the foregoing pages. It is that which took us to Sumatra in seach of the titan arum. We could not possibly have succceeded in that quest without the guidance and advice of Dr James Symon of San Francisco for whom this amazing species has been an obsession for many years.

Lastly I must thank Dr Kingsley Dixon and Professor Gren Lucas, both of whom were extraordinarily generous with their time and learning in commenting on early drafts of this book.

THE PRIVATE LIFE OF PLANTS

The Television Team

Executive Producer
Mike Salisbury

Producers
Neil Nightingale
Keith Scholey

Assistant Producer
Neil Lucas

Researcher
Mark Flowers

Unit Manager
Cynthia Connolly

Production Assistants
Pamela Jackson
Lisa Pearce
Elizabeth Toogood

Production Secretary
Bernadette JohnLewis

Production Office
Fiona Harrington
Anthony Lee
Catherine Mockridge
Martin Whatley

Field Assistants
Chris Birkinshaw
Isidro Chacon
Arno Grabner-Meyer
Phil Hurrell
Anton Pauw
Andrew Small

Music
Richard Lewis

Graphics
Mick Connaire

Film Editors
Tim Coope
Martin Elsbury
Jo Payne

Assistant Film Editors
Krissy Balaam
Norman Burgess
Angela Groves
Emma Jones

Video Editors
Ian Haynes
Steve Olive

Photography
Neil Bromhall
Richard Ganniclifft
Richard Kirby
Tim Shepherd
Gavin Thurston

Additional Photography
David Barlow
Natasha Breed
Barrie Britton
Glen Carruthers
Rod Clarke
Walt Deas
Mike deGruy
Trevor De Kock

Chris Doncaster
Steve Downer
Bill Duyck
Geoff Gartside
John Hadfield
Roy Hunt
Mike Lemmon
Ian McCarthy
Hugh Miles
Stephen Mills
Owen Newman
Michael Pitts
David Rasmussen
Peter Smithson
Jonathan Watts
John Waters
Kim Wolhuter

Photographic Assistants
Mike England
Tim Howell
Simon Wagen

Sound Recordist
Trevor Gosling

Additional Sound
Lyndon Bird
Kevin Meredith
Jeff Taylor

Dubbing Editor
Lucy Rutherford

Dubbing Mixers
Martyn Harries
Peter Hicks

SOURCES OF PHOTOGRAPHS

We are most grateful to the many organisations and individual photographers who have provided the photographs in this book, as listed below.

Frontispiece David Attenborough; **10** Garden Matters (John Feltwell); **12** Garden Matters (John Feltwell); **14** Neil Lucas; **15** Martin Cheek; **16** Aquila (Abraham Cardwell); **17** NHPA (Stephen Dalton); **18** Jacana (Michel Viard); **19** Heather Angel; **20** Oxford Scientific Films (Harold Taylor); **21** Heather Angel; **22** Heather Angel; **23** Oxford Scientific Films (G.I. Bernard); **24** Anton Pauw; **26** Okapia (Masahiro Iijima); **27** Michael Pitts; **28** Oxford Scientific Films (Michael Fogden); **30** Gerald Cubitt; **33** Planet Earth Pictures (André Bärtschi); **34** Neil Lucas; **36** Bruce Coleman (Hans Reinhard); **37** A-Z Botanical Collection (Dicon J. Joseph); **39** *all* Mitsuhiko Imamori; **40** Gordon Dickson; **41** Tim Shepherd; **42** Bruce Coleman (Frans Lanting); **43** NHPA (E.A. James); **44** Garden Matters (John Feltwell); **45** Oxford Scientific Films (Harold Taylor); **46** Oxford Scientific Films (G.I. Bernard); **47** Günter Ziesler; **48** *above left* Oxford Scientific Films (Harold Taylor), *above right* Garden Matters (John Feltwell), *lower left* Planet Earth Pictures (André Bärtschi), *lower right* Bruce Coleman (Alain Compost); **49** Bios (R. Seitre); **50** Bruce Coleman (Fred Bruemmer); **53** Earth Images (Terry Domico); **55** Bios (Denis Bringard); **56** Ardea (Jean Paul Ferrero); **57** *both* Bruce Coleman (Jeremy Grayson); **59** *all* Mitsuhiko Imamori; **60** Philip Devries; **62** Keith Scholey; **63** Bruce Coleman (Günter Ziesler); **64** *above* K & B News Foto (Giuliano Valsecchi), *below* Bruce Coleman (Kim Taylor); **65** Aquila (A.J. Bond); **66** Garden Matters (John Feltwell); **67** Premaphotos Wildlife; **69** *both* Jacana (Jean Paul Hervy); **71** FLPA (E. & D. Hosking); **73** Oxford Scientific Films (Paul Franklin); **75** Photo Researchers (Jeff Lepore); **76** Photo Researchers (Jeff Lepore); **77** Michael Salisbury; **79** *all* Garden Matters (John Feltwell); **80** *above left, below right* Bruce Coleman (Gerald Cubitt), *above right* A-Z Botanical Collection (Jiri Loun), *below left* Oxford Scientific Films (Kjell B. Sandved); **81** Bruce Coleman (Alain Compost); **82** *all* Bruce Coleman (Jane Burton); **83** Earth Images (Terry Domico); **84** Oxford Scientific Films (Sean Morris); **85** Ardea (P. Morris); **87** NHPA (John Shaw); **88** Bios (Henry Philippe); **89** Bruce Coleman (P. Clement); **90-1** Bruce Coleman (Jules Cowan); **93** Oxford Scientific Films (M.P.L. Fogden); **94** *1, 3, 5, 7,* Okapia (Manfred P. Kage) *6, 8, 10,* Phototake (Denis Kunkel) *2, 4, 12,* Phototake (Jean Claude Revy) *9, 11,* Microscopix (Andrew Syred); **97** NHPA (Stephen Dalton); **98** Bruce Coleman (Pekka Helo); **101** Peter Gasson; **102** *both* Premaphotos Wildlife; **103** *both* Heather Angel; **104** Premaphotos Wildlife; **105** Planet Earth Pictures (Steve Hopkin); **106** Mitsuhiko Imamori; **107** *both* Mitsuhiko Imamori; **109** Oxford Scientific Films (D.H. Thompson); **110** Oxford Scientific Films (D.H. Thompson); **111** Premaphotos Wildlife; **112-3** A. Whitaker; **114** Oxford Scientific Films (G.I. Bernard); **115** Jan Aldenhoven; **116** Oxford Scientific Films (Bert Wells); **118** Aquila

(Wayne Lankinen); **120** Biofotos (Andrew Henley); **123** Okapia (D.J. Howell); **125** David Attenborough; **126** *both* Claudia Gack; **127** *all* Claudia Gack/H.F. Paulus; **128** *above* H.F. Paulus, *below* Claudia Gack; **129** Mitsuhiko Imamori; **130** *both* Mitsuhiko Imamori; **133** Oxford Scientific Films (Sean Morris); **135** David Attenborough; **137** Neil Lucas; **138** James Symon; **141** ABPL (Anthony Bannister); **143** NHPA (Anthony Bannister); **145** *above* Aquila (C.S. Milkins), *below* Garden Matters (John Feltwell); **146** Bruce Coleman (Jane Burton); **148** Garden-Matters (John Feltwell); **150** Planet Earth Pictures (Richard Coomber); **152** Heather Angel; **153** Bruce Coleman (P. Evans); **154-5** FLPA (M.J. Thomas); **157** *all* Bruce Coleman (Kim Taylor); **159** J. Allan Cash; **160** Photo Researchers (Jeff Lepore); **161** Anton Pauw; **162** Martin Cheek; **163** Oxford Scientific Films (John Paling);164 John Dransfield; **165** Günter Ziesler; **167** *above* Michael Pitts, *below* Photo Researchers (Paul A. Zahl); **168** Bruce Coleman (Luiz Claudio Marigo); **169** Okapia (Ted Mead); **171** Gerald Cubitt; **173** Ardea (Jean Paul Ferrero); **175** Gordon Dickson; **176** Mantis Wildlife (Densey Clyne); **177** Bruce Coleman (M.P.L. Fogden); **178** *above left* Ardea (Jean Paul Ferrero), *above right* Premaphotos Wildlife, *below left* NHPA (Haroldo Palo Jr), *below right* Mantis Wildlife (Densey Clyne); **179** Phototake (Carolina Biological Supply Co.); **181** Earth Images (Terry Domico); **182** *above* Photo Researchers (Jim Zipp), *below* Heather Angel; **185** A-Z Botanical Collection (Irene Windridge); **187** Barnaby's Picture Library (A.J. Fox); **189** S.D. Hopper; **190** *left* Ardea (Jean Paul Ferrero), *right* Ardea (B. Sage); **191** David Attenborough; **192** *all* Auscape (Jean Paul Ferrero); **195** Photo Researchers (Sven D. Lindblad); **197** Planet Earth Pictures (John Eastcott and Yva Momatiuk); **198** Georgette Douwma; **199** Oxford Scientific Films (Peter Parks); **200** Heather Angel; **202** Michael Pitts; **203** Planet Earth Pictures (Linda Pitkin); **204** Ardea (Ron and Valerie Taylor); **207** *above* Mitsuhiko Imamori, *below* Oxford Scientific Films (Philip K. Sharpe); **208** Premaphotos Wildlife; **210** *both* Bruce Coleman (Alain Compost); **211** Bruce Coleman (Alain Compost); **212** Heather Angel; **215** *above* Fred Bruemmer, *below* Premaphotos Wildlife; **216** Premaphotos Wildlife; **217** Phototake (Carolina Biological Supply Co.); **218** Premaphotos Wildlife; **221** Phototake (Carolina Biological Supply Co.); **223** Papilio (Bryan Knox); **224** Oxford Scientific Films (Tom Leach); **225** Oxford Scientific Films (J.A.L. Cooke); **227** David Attenborough; **229** Photo Researchers (Gilbert Grant); **230** Jan Aldenhoven; **231** Jan Aldenhoven; **232** Glen Carruthers; **233** Garden Matters (John Feltwell); **235** Oriol Alamany; **236** *both* Mitsuhiko Imamori; **237** *both* Mitsuhiko Imamori; **238-9** Mitsuhiko Imamori; **240** Bios (A. Visage/Alain Compost); **241** Mitsuhiko Imamori; **242** Bios (Alain Compost); **245** Fred Bruemmer; **247** Earth Images (David Denning); **248** Michael Salisbury; **249** Michael Salisbury; **250** Fred Bruemmer; **251** Oriol Alamany; **252** Bruce Coleman (Hans Reinhard); **253** Bruce Coleman (Hans Reinhard); **254** Christopher Grey-Wilson; **256** Auscape (Dennis Harding); **257** David Attenborough; **258-9** Oxford Scientific Films (David W. Breed); **261** Neil Lucas; **262** Neil Lucas; **264** Oxford Scientific Films (Michael Fogden); **266** Neil Nightingale; **267** Fred Bruemmer; **268** Planet Earth Pictures (Nick Garbutt); **270-1** FLPA (Koos Delport); **272** Neil Nightingale;

273 *all* Premaphotos Wildlife; **274** Gerald Cubitt; **276-7** Gerald Cubitt; **279** Jan Aldenhoven; **280-1** Geo (Uwe George); **283** David Attenborough; **284** David Attenborough; **285** Geo (Uwe George); **286** Jan Aldenhoven; **287** NHPA (G.I. Bernard); **288** Bios (M. and C. Denis-Huot); **289** Photo Researchers (Jany Sauvanet); **290** Photo Researchers (J.P. Vuillomenet); **291** Mitsuhiko Imamori; **292** Oxford Scientific Films (David Thompson); **293** *both* Oxford Scientific Films (Sean Morris); **294** Bruce Coleman (John Shaw); **296-7** Planet Earth Pictures (Peter Scoones); **299** Premaphotos Wildlife; **300** Planet Earth Pictures (Keith Scholey); **301** Barnaby's Picture Library (S. and L. Frawley); **303** Planet Earth Pictures (Georgette Douwma); **304** Heather Angel; **305** *above* Oxford Scientific Films (David Shale), *below* Oxford Scientific Films (Z. Leszczynski); **307** Okapia (A. & H-F. Michler).

INDEX

The names of the plants used in the text are here accompanied by their scientific names, which identify the plant more precisely than do the English names. Numerals in **bold** type indicate illustrations.